# THE WORDS OF CHRIST

# THE
# WORDS
# OF
# CHRIST

EDITED BY

DALE SALWAK

NEW WORLD LIBRARY
NOVATO, CALIFORNIA

From the
Library of:

The John Fox Family

New World Library
14 Pamaron Way
Novato, CA 94949

Cover Design: Greg Wittrock
Text Design & Typography: Linda Corwin

Library of Congress Cataloging-in-Publication Data
Salwak, Dale.
The words of Christ / edited by Dale Salwak.
p.    cm
ISBN 1-88032-84-8 (cloth : alk. paper)
1. Jesus Christ--Words.        I. Title

BT306.S324    1996                    96-2670
225.5'2--dc20                          CIP

First printing, February 1996
ISBN 0-880032-84-8
Printed in the U.S.A. on acid-free paper
Distributed by Publishers Group West
10  9  8  7  6  5  4  3  2  1

# CONTENTS

# Contents

# INTRODUCTION

*Heaven and earth will pass away,*
*but my words will not pass away.*

The words of Christ leap across the changing centuries because He speaks to the unchanging needs of the hearts of men and women everywhere. Where have we come from? Why are we here? Where are we going? Christ addresses all this and more, not as an end in itself, but as a means of bringing us ultimately to an intimate and satisfying knowledge of God and His irrevocable will for us and our world.

Christ's words, says fifteenth-century Dutch ecclesiastic Thomas à Kempis, are designed to "fire the heart and lighten the understanding, foster contrition and bring comfort," and His plan of renewal and redemption is the fundamental source of unity in the teachings, running like a golden thread throughout His discourses, parables, and maxims. No matter our temperament, experience, or spiritual outlook, we owe Him a hearing.

The word Christ (from the Greek, *Christos*) originates in the Hebrew *Messias* (Messiah) or "anointed one." His mission on earth, He said, was to reveal "as it is in heaven" the kingdom of God, the spiritual realm of perfection, and to establish in our hearts and minds forever the reign and sovereignty of God. "Repent," he says, "for the kingdom of God is at hand." His audience, however, did not always understand or believe Him; and during His life on earth, as now, hearers are divided as they encounter His words.

Yet the message has endured and, if we are willing to listen, speaks to us today. When He emphasizes, for example, the blessings of humility, poverty of spirit, sorrow for sin, gentleness, forgiveness of injustice, mercy, purity of heart, and peace and joy in the midst of persecution, these are not safe generalizations by which we can engineer a happy life. Rather, they are intended to startle us out of our inherent narrow vision and direct us into a new way of thinking and acting. "The words that I have spoken to you are spirit and life," He says with authority. "If you abide in me, and my words abide in you, ask whatever you wish, and it will be done for you."

Other than one scene in the Gospel According to John (8:6) in which Christ wrote something in the sand for the benefit of His disciples, He taught only by the spoken word, in Aramaic; several decades later, eyewitnesses translated and recorded His words (with a few exceptions) into the Greek *koine* of popular speech — from which we derive our English translations today.

So distinct are these words that if they were given to us mingled with the words of others, such as Socrates or Buddha or Confucius, we would be able to select His teachings from the whole — just as anyone with a trained ear for verse could pick out separate lines of William Shakespeare from a general collection of poetry. Turn to His words, says Erasmus, the great biblical scholar of Rotterdam, and there you will find "Christ Himself . . . in an intimacy so close that He would be less visible to you if He stood before your eyes."

Sometimes, I think, the teachings *about* Christ have somewhat overshadowed the teachings *of* Christ. Cutting through the lens of history and hundreds of years of commentaries and controversies, therefore, I have distilled from the New Revised Standard Version (NRSV) the essence of what He said and arranged His teachings thematically. My selections come from the four canonical Gospels (known to many as the books of

Matthew, Mark, Luke, and John), the Acts of the Apostles, 1 and 2 Corinthians, and Revelation. It is hoped that working through His words in this way will become as enlightening and thoroughly absorbing an experience for the reader as it has been for me. New streams of light may come in through a hundred windows; familiar passages might take on new meanings; and sometimes a very old question will be answered with amazing ease. His words can speak to us personally, opening up our understanding right where we are and regardless of who we are. Indeed, Christ's words can be like a mirror inviting us to look deeply within ourselves. And that is when life truly begins!

"I am the light of the world," Christ says. "Whoever follows me will never walk in darkness but will have the light of life."

The words that follow here have helped many generations of readers find their way in the darkness. May their light guide our journey as well.

Dale Salwak
Citrus College
Glendora, CA

# THE
# WORDS
# OF
# CHRIST

# THE
# MISSION
# OF
# CHRIST

# WORDS
## OF
## ASSURANCE

Very truly, I tell you, before Abraham was, I am.

– JOHN 8:58

I am the root and the descendant of David, the bright morning star.

– REVELATION 22:16

If you abide in me, and my words abide in you, ask for whatever you wish, and it will be done for you. My Father is glorified by this, that you bear much fruit and become my disciples.

– JOHN 15:7-8

Whoever has seen me has seen the Father. . . . The words that I say to you I do not speak on my own; but the Father who dwells in me does his works. Believe me that I am in the Father and the Father is in me; but if you do not, then believe me because of the works themselves.

– JOHN 14:9-11

My teaching is not mine but his who sent me. Anyone who resolves to do the will of God will know whether the teaching is from God or whether I am speaking on my own. Those who speak on their own seek their own glory; but the one who seeks the glory of him who sent him is true, and there is nothing false in him.

– JOHN 7:16-18

If I glorify myself, my glory is nothing. It is my Father who glorifies me, he of whom you say, "He is our God," though you do not know him. But I know him; if I would say that I do not know him, I would be a liar like you. But I do know him and I keep his word. Your ancestor Abraham rejoiced that he would see my day; he saw it and was glad.

– JOHN 8:54-56

Very truly, I tell you, the Son can do nothing on his own, but only what he sees the Father doing; for whatever the Father does, the Son does likewise. The Father loves the Son and shows him all that he himself is doing; and he will show him greater works than these, so that you will be astonished. Indeed, just as the Father raises the dead and gives them life, so also the Son gives life to whomever he wishes. The Father judges no one but has given all judgment to the Son, so that all may honor the Son just as they honor the Father.     – JOHN 5:19-23

All things have been handed over to me by my Father; and no one knows the Son except the Father, and no one knows the Father except the Son and anyone to whom the Son chooses to reveal him.

    – MATTHEW 11:27; LUKE 10:22

God is spirit, and those who worship him must worship in spirit and truth. . . . I am he [the Christ], the one who is speaking to you.     – JOHN 4:24, 26

Those who are well have no need of a physician, but those who are sick; I have come to call [to repentance] not the righteous but sinners.

    – MARK 2:17; MATTHEW 9:12-13; LUKE 5:31-32

For the Son of Man came to seek out and to save the lost.     – LUKE 19:10

I was sent only to the lost sheep of the house of Israel.

    – MATTHEW 15:24

Very truly, I tell you, anyone who does not enter the sheepfold by the gate but climbs in by another way is a thief and a bandit. The one who enters by the gate is the shepherd of the sheep. The gatekeeper opens the gate for him, and the sheep hear his voice. He calls his own sheep by name and leads them out. When he has brought out all his own, he goes ahead of them, and the sheep follow him because they know his voice. They will not follow a stranger, but they will run from him because they do not know the voice of strangers.

– JOHN 10:1-5; CF. 7-10

I am the good shepherd. The good shepherd lays down his life for the sheep. The hired hand, who is not the shepherd and does not own the sheep, sees the wolf coming and leaves the sheep and runs away — and the wolf snatches them and scatters them. The hired hand runs away because a hired hand does not care for the sheep. I am the good shepherd. I know my own and my own know me, just as the Father knows me and I know the Father. And I lay down my life for the sheep. I have other sheep that do not belong to this fold. I must bring them also, and they will listen to my voice. So there will be one flock, one shepherd. For this reason the Father loves me, because I lay down my life in order to take it up again. No one takes it from me, but I lay it down of my own accord. I have power to lay it down, and I have power to take it up again. I have received this command from my Father.

– JOHN 10:11-18

My sheep hear my voice. I know them, and they follow me. I give them eternal life, and they will never perish. No one will snatch them out of my hand. What my Father has given me is greater than all else, and no one can snatch it out of the Father's hand. The Father and I are one.

— JOHN 10:27-30

Do not fear those who kill the body but cannot kill the soul; rather fear him who can destroy both soul and body in hell. Are not two sparrows sold for a penny? Yet not one of them will fall to the ground apart from your Father. And even the hairs of your head are all counted. So do not be afraid; you are of more value than many sparrows.

— MATTHEW 10:28-31; LUKE 12:4-7

But not a hair of your head will perish. By your endurance you will gain your souls.

— LUKE 21:18-19

I can do nothing on my own. As I hear, I judge; and my judgment is just, because I seek to do not my own will but the will of him who sent me.

If I testify about myself, my testimony is not true. There is another who testifies on my behalf, and I know that his testimony to me is true. You sent messengers to John [the Baptist], and he testified to the truth. Not that I accept such human testimony, but I say these things so that you may be saved. He was a burning and shining lamp, and you were willing to rejoice for a while in his light. But I have a testimony greater than John's. The works that the Father has given me to complete, the very works that I am doing, testify on my behalf that the Father has sent me. And the Father who sent me has himself testified on my behalf.

– JOHN 5:30-37

Even if I testify on my own behalf, my testimony is valid because I know where I have come from and where I am going, but you do not know where I come from or where I am going. You judge by human standards; I judge no one. Yet even if I do judge, my judgment is valid; for it is not I alone who judge, but I and the Father who sent me. In your law it is written that the testimony of two witnesses is valid. I testify on my own behalf, and the Father who sent me testifies on my behalf.

– JOHN 8:14-18

When you have lifted up the Son of Man, then you will realize that I am he, and that I do nothing on my own, but I speak these things as the Father instructed me. And the one who sent me is with me; he has not left me alone, for I always do what is pleasing to him.

– JOHN 8:28-29

I have shown you many good works from the Father.

For which of these are you going to stone me?... Is it not written in your law, "I said, you are gods"? If those to whom the word of God came were called "gods" — and the scripture cannot be annulled — can you say that the one whom the Father has sanctified and sent into the world is blaspheming because I said, "I am God's Son"? If I am not doing the works of my Father, then do not believe me. But if I do them, even though you do not believe me, believe the works, so that you may know and understand that the Father is in me and I am in the Father.

– JOHN 10:32, 34-38

Do not let your hearts be troubled. Believe in God, believe also in me. In my Father's house there are many dwelling places. If it were not so, would I have told you that I go to prepare a place for you? And if I go and prepare a place for you, I will come again and will take you to myself, so that where I am, there you may be also. And you know the way to the place where I am going.

– JOHN 14:1-4

I am the way, and the truth, and the life. No one comes to the Father except through me. If you know me, you will know my Father also. From now on you do know him and have seen him.

– JOHN 14:6-7

I have food to eat that you do not know about.... My

food is to do the will of him who sent me and to complete his work. Do you not say, "Four months more, then comes the harvest"? But I tell you, look around you, and see how the fields are ripe for harvesting. The reaper is already receiving wages and is gathering fruit for eternal life, so that sower and reaper may rejoice together. For here the saying holds true, "One sows and another reaps." I sent you to reap that for which you did not labor. Others have labored, and you have entered into their labor.

– JOHN 4:32, 34-38

Very truly, I tell you, it was not Moses who gave you the bread from heaven, but it is my Father who gives you the true bread from heaven. For the bread of God is that which comes down from heaven and gives life to the world.

– JOHN 6:32-33

I am the bread of life. Whoever comes to me will never be hungry, and whoever believes in me will never be thirsty. But I said to you that you have seen me and yet do not believe. Everything that the Father gives me will come to me, and anyone who comes to me I will never drive away; for I have come down from heaven, not to do my own will, but the will of him who sent me. And this is the will of him who sent me, that I should lose nothing of all that he has given me, but raise it up on the last day. This is indeed the will of my Father, that all who see the Son and believe in him may have eternal life; and I will raise them up on the last day.     — JOHN 6:35-40

Very truly, I tell you, whoever believes has eternal life. I am the bread of life. Your ancestors ate the manna in the wilderness, and they died. This is the bread that comes down from heaven, so that one may eat of it and not die. I am the living bread that came down from heaven. Whoever eats of this bread will live forever; and the bread that I will give for the life of the world is my flesh. . . .

Very truly, I tell you, unless you eat the flesh of the Son of Man and drink his blood, you have no life in you. Those who eat my flesh and drink my blood have eternal life, and I will raise them up on the last day; for my flesh is true food and my blood is true drink. Those who eat my flesh and drink my blood abide in me, and I in them. Just as the living Father sent me, and I live because of the Father, so whoever eats me will live because of me. This is the bread that came down from heaven, not like that which your ancestors ate, and they died. But the one who eats this bread will live forever.

— JOHN 6:47-51, 53-58

Everyone who drinks of this water [at the well] will be

thirsty again, but those who drink of the water that I will give them will never be thirsty. The water that I will give will become in them a spring of water gushing up to eternal life.

— JOHN 4:13-14; CF. 4:10

For God so loved the world that he gave his only Son, so that everyone who believes in him may not perish but may have eternal life.

Indeed, God did not send the Son into the world to condemn the world, but in order that the world might be saved through him. Those who believe in him are not condemned; but those who do not believe are condemned already, because they have not believed in the name of the only Son of God.

— JOHN 3:16-18

Very truly, I tell you, the one who believes in me will also do the works that I do and, in fact, will do greater works than these, because I am going to the Father. I will do whatever you ask in my name, so that the Father may be glorified in the Son. If in my name you ask me for anything, I will do it.

— JOHN 14:12-14

If you love me, you will keep my commandments. And I will ask the Father, and he will give you another Advocate [the Holy Spirit], to be with you forever. This is the Spirit of truth, whom the world cannot receive, because it neither sees him nor knows him. You know him, because he abides with you, and he will be in you.

— JOHN 14:15-17

Those who love me will keep my word, and my Father will love them, and we will come to them and make our home with them. Whoever does not love me does not keep my words; and the word that you hear is not mine, but is from the Father who sent me.

— JOHN 14:23-24

Whoever believes in me believes not in me but in him who sent me. And whoever sees me sees him who sent me. I have come as light into the world, so that everyone who believes in me should not remain in the darkness. I do not judge anyone who hears my words and does not keep them, for I came not to judge the world, but to save the world. The one who rejects me and does not receive my word has a judge; on the last day the word that I have spoken will serve as judge, for I have not spoken on my own, but the Father who sent me has himself given me a commandment about what to say and what to speak. And I know that his commandment is eternal life. What I speak, therefore, I speak just as the Father has told me.

— JOHN 12:44-50

Who is my mother, and who are my brothers?... Here

are my mother and my brothers! For whoever does the will of my Father in heaven is my brother and sister and mother. — Matthew 12:48-50; Mark 3:33-35; Luke 8:21

Whoever welcomes this child in my name welcomes me, and whoever welcomes me welcomes the one who sent me; for the least among all of you is the greatest.

— Luke 9:48; John 13:20

Again, truly I tell you, if two of you agree on earth about anything you ask, it will be done for you by my Father in heaven. For where two or three are gathered in my name, I am there among them. — Matthew 18:19-20

Is there anyone among you who, if your child asks for bread, will give a stone? Or if the child asks for a fish, will give a snake? If you then, who are evil, know how to give good gifts to your children, how much more will your Father in heaven give good things to those who ask him! — Matthew 7:9-11; Luke 11:11-13

No one can come to me unless drawn by the Father who sent me; and I will raise that person up on the last day. It is written in the prophets, "And they shall all be taught by God." Everyone who has heard and learned from the Father comes to me. Not that anyone has seen the Father except the one who is from God;

he has seen the Father.

— JOHN 6:44-46

Does this offend you? Then what if you were to see the Son of Man ascending to where he was before? It is the spirit that gives life; the flesh is useless. The words that I have spoken to you are spirit and life. But among you there are some who do not believe. . . . For this reason I have told you that no one can come to me unless it is granted by the Father.

— JOHN 6:61-65

And as for the resurrection of the dead, have you not read what was said to you by God, "I am the God of Abraham, the God of Isaac, and the God of Jacob"? He is God not of the dead, but of the living.

— MATTHEW 22:31-32; LUKE 20:37-38; MARK 12:26-27

Come to me, all you that are weary and are carrying heavy burdens, and I will give you rest. Take my yoke upon you, and learn from me; for I am gentle and humble in heart, and you will find rest for your souls. For my yoke is easy, and my burden is light.

— MATTHEW 11:28-30

Heaven and earth will pass away, but my words will not pass away. — MATTHEW 24:35; MARK 13:31; LUKE 21:33

Do not think that I have come to abolish the law or the

prophets; I have come not to abolish but to fulfill. For truly I tell you, until heaven and earth pass away, not one letter, not one stroke of a letter, will pass from the law until all is accomplished.

— Matthew 5:17-18; Luke 16:17

Go and tell John [the Baptist] what you have seen and heard: the blind receive their sight, the lame walk, the lepers are cleansed, the deaf hear, the dead are raised, the poor have good news brought to them. And blessed is anyone who takes no offense at me.

— Luke 7:22-23; Matthew 11:4-6

I do not have a demon; but I honor my Father. . . . Yet I do not seek my own glory; there is one who seeks it and he is the judge. Very truly, I tell you, whoever keeps my word will never see death.

— John 8:49-51

I have much to say about you and much to condemn; but the one who sent me is true, and I declare to the world what I have heard from him.

— John 8:26

I have said these things to you while I am still with you. But the Advocate, the Holy Spirit, whom the Father will send in my name, will teach you everything, and remind you of all that I have said to you.

— John 14:25-26

Blessed . . . are those who hear the word of God and obey it!
— LUKE 11:28

My grace is sufficient for you, for power is made perfect in weakness.
— 2 CORINTHIANS 12:9

Everyone then who hears these words of mine and acts on them will be like a wise man who built his house on rock. The rain fell, the floods came, and the winds blew and beat on that house, but it did not fall, because it had been founded on rock.

— MATTHEW 7:24-25; LUKE 6:47-48

I still have many things to say to you, but you cannot bear them now. When the Spirit of truth comes, he will guide you into all the truth; for he will not speak on his own, but will speak whatever he hears, and he will declare to you the things that are to come. He will glorify me, because he will take what is mine and declare it to you. All that the Father has is mine. For this reason I said that he will take what is mine and declare it to you.
— JOHN 16:12-15

I have made your [the Father's] name known to those whom you gave me from the world. They were yours, and you gave them to me, and they have kept your word. Now they know that everything you have given me is from you; for the words that you gave to me I have given to them, and they have received them and know in truth that I came from you; and they have believed that you sent me. I am asking on their behalf; I am not asking on behalf of the world, but on behalf of those whom you gave me, because they are yours. All mine are yours, and yours are mine, and I have been glorified in them.

– JOHN 17:6-10

And now I am no longer in the world, but they are in the world, and I am coming to you. Holy Father, protect them in your name that you have given me, so that they may be one, as we are one. While I was with them, I protected them in your name that you have given me. I guarded them, and not one of them was lost except the one destined to be lost, so that the scripture might be fulfilled. But now I am coming to you, and I speak these things in the world so that they may have my joy made complete in themselves. I have given them your word, and the world has hated them because they do not belong to the world, just as I do not belong to the world. I am not asking you to take them out of the world, but I ask you to protect them from the evil one. They do not belong to the world, just as I do not belong to the world. Sanctify them in the truth; your word is truth. As you have sent me into the world, so I have sent them into the world. And for their sakes I sanctify myself, so that they also may be sanctified in truth.

– JOHN 17:11-19

I ask not only on behalf of these, but also on behalf of those who will believe in me through their word, that they may all be one. As you, Father, are in me and I am in you, may they also be in us, so that the world may believe that you have sent me. The glory that you have given me I have given them, so that they may be one, as we are one, I in them and you in me, that they may become completely one, so that the world may know that you have sent me and have loved them even as you have loved me. Father, I desire that those also, whom you have given me, may be with me where I am, to see my glory, which you have given me because you loved me before the foundation of the world.

– JOHN 17:20-24

Righteous Father, the world does not know you, but I know you; and these know that you have sent me. I made your name known to them, and I will make it known, so that the love with which you have loved me may be in them, and I in them.

– JOHN 17:25-26

I thank you, Father, Lord of heaven and earth, because you have hidden these things from the wise and the intelligent and have revealed them to infants; yes,

Father, for such was your gracious will.

— MATTHEW 11:25-26; LUKE 10:21

My Father is still working, and I also am working [giving life and judging evil].

— JOHN 5:17

# FULFILLING
# THE
# FATHER'S WILL

[As a child of twelve:]

Why were you searching for me? Did you not know that I must be in my Father's house [the temple]?

— LUKE 2:49

[As a man of thirty reading from the prophet Isaiah:] "The Spirit of the Lord is upon me, because he has anointed me to bring good news to the poor. He has sent me to proclaim release to the captives and recovery of sight to the blind, to let the oppressed go free, to proclaim the year of the Lord's favor." . . . Today this scripture has been fulfilled in your hearing.

— LUKE 4:18-19, 21

I must proclaim the good news of the kingdom of God to the other cities also; for I was sent for this purpose.

— LUKE 4:43; MARK 1:38

Let it [His baptism by John the Baptist] be so now; for it is proper for us in this way to fulfill all righteousness.

— MATTHEW 3:15

. . . John baptized with water, but you will be baptized with the Holy Spirit not many days from now.

— ACTS 1:5

What did you go out into the wilderness to look at? A reed shaken by the wind? What then did you go out to see? Someone dressed in soft robes? Look, those who put on fine clothing and live in luxury are in royal palaces. What then did you go out to see? A prophet? Yes, I tell you, and more than a prophet. This [John the Baptist] is the one about whom it is written,

"See, I am sending my messenger ahead of you [Jesus], who will prepare your way before you."

— LUKE 7:24-27; MATTHEW 11:7-10; CF. MARK 1:2

Truly I tell you, among those born of women no one has arisen greater than John the Baptist; yet the least in the kingdom of heaven is greater than he. From the days of John the Baptist until now the kingdom of heaven has suffered violence, and the violent take it by force. For all the prophets and the law prophesied until John came; and if you are willing to accept it, he is Elijah who is to come. Let anyone with ears listen!

– MATTHEW 11:11-15; LUKE 7:28

Elijah is indeed coming first to restore all things. How then is it written about the Son of Man, that he is to go through many sufferings and be treated with contempt? But I tell you that Elijah [in the person of John the Baptist] has come, and they did to him whatever they pleased, as it is written about him.

– MARK 9:12-13; MATTHEW 17:11-12

To what then will I compare the people of this generation, and what are they like? They are like children sitting in the marketplace and calling to one another,

"We played the flute for you, and you did not dance; we wailed, and you did not weep."

For John the Baptist has come eating no bread and drinking no wine, and you say, "He has a demon"; the Son of Man has come eating and drinking, and you say, "Look, a glutton and a drunkard, a friend of tax collectors and sinners!" Nevertheless, wisdom is vindicated by all her children.

– LUKE 7:31-35; MATTHEW 11:16-19

Who do the crowds say that I am? [The disciples

answered, "John the Baptist; but others, Elijah; and still others, that one of the ancient prophets has arisen."] . . . But who do you say that I am? [Peter answered, "The Christ of God."]

— LUKE 9:18-20; MATTHEW 16:13-16; MARK 8:27-29

The Son of Man must undergo great suffering, and be rejected by the elders, chief priests, and scribes, and be killed, and on the third day be raised.

— LUKE 9:22, 44; MATTHEW 17:22-23; MARK 9:31

Get up and do not be afraid. . . . Tell no one about the vision [of Moses and Elijah with Jesus] until after the Son of Man has been raised from the dead.

— MATTHEW 17:7, 9

Destroy this temple [of my body], and in three days I will raise it up. — JOHN 2:19

I will be with you a little while longer, and then I am going to him who sent me. You will search for me, but you will not find me; and where I am, you cannot come.

— JOHN 7:33-34

A little while, and you will no longer see me, and again a little while, and you will see me. . . . Very truly, I tell you, you will weep and mourn, but the world will rejoice; you will have pain, but your pain will turn into joy. When a woman is in labor, she has pain, because her hour has come. But when her child is born, she no longer remembers the anguish because of the joy of having brought a human being into the world. So you have pain now; but I will see you again, and your hearts will rejoice, and no one will take your joy from you. On that day you will ask nothing of me.

— John 16:16, 20-23

You know that after two days the Passover is coming, and the Son of Man will be handed over to be crucified.

— Matthew 26:2

I will not leave you orphaned; I am coming to you. In a little while the world will no longer see me, but you will see me; because I live, you also will live. On that day you will know that I am in my Father, and you in me, and I in you.

— John 14:18-20

My time has not yet come, but your time is always here. The world cannot hate you, but it hates me because I testify against it that its works are evil. Go to the festival yourselves. I am not going to this festival, for my time has not yet fully come.

— John 7:6-8; cf. 2:4

The hour has come for the Son of Man to be glorified. Very truly, I tell you, unless a grain of wheat falls into the earth and dies, it remains just a single grain; but if it dies, it bears much fruit. Those who love their life lose it, and those who hate their life in this world will keep it for eternal life. Whoever serves me must follow me, and where I am, there will my servant be also. Whoever serves me, the Father will honor.

– JOHN 12:23-26

I have said these things to you in figures of speech. The hour is coming when I will no longer speak to you in figures, but will tell you plainly of the Father. On that day you will ask in my name. I do not say to you that I will ask the Father on your behalf; for the Father himself loves you, because you have loved me and have believed that I came from God. I came from the Father, and have come into the world; again, I am leaving the world and going to the Father.

– JOHN 16:25-28

Do you now believe? The hour is coming, indeed it has come, when you will be scattered, each one to his home, and you will leave me alone. Yet I am not alone because the Father is with me. I have said this to you, so that in me you may have peace. In the world you face persecution. But take courage; I have conquered the world!

– JOHN 16:31-33

This voice [of the Father] has come for your sake, not for mine. Now is the judgment of this world; now the ruler of this world [Satan] will be driven out. And I, when I am lifted up from the earth, will draw all people to myself.

— JOHN 12:30-32; CF. 13:36

Peace I leave with you; my peace I give to you. I do not give to you as the world gives. Do not let your hearts be troubled, and do not let them be afraid. You heard me say to you, "I am going away, and I am coming to you." If you loved me, you would rejoice that I am going to the Father, because the Father is greater than I. And now I have told you this before it occurs, so that when it does occur, you may believe. I will no longer talk much with you, for the ruler of this world [Satan] is coming. He has no power over me; but I do as the Father has commanded me, so that the world may know that I love the Father. Rise, let us go on our way.

— JOHN 14:27-31

The wedding guests cannot fast while the bridegroom is with them, can they? As long as they have the bridegroom with them, they cannot fast. The days will come when the bridegroom is taken away from them, and then they will fast on that day.

— MARK 2:19-20; LUKE 5:34-35; MATTHEW 9:15

See, we are going up to Jerusalem, and the Son of Man will be handed over to the chief priests and the scribes, and they will condemn him over to death; then they will hand him over to the Gentiles; they will mock him, and spit upon him, and flog him, and kill him; and after three days he will rise again.

— MARK 10:33-34; MATTHEW 20:18-19; LUKE 18:31-33

Go into the village ahead of you, and immediately as you enter it, you will find tied there a colt that has never been ridden; untie it and bring it. If anyone says to you, "Why are you doing this?" just say this, "The Lord needs it and will send it back here immediately."

— MARK 11:2-3; MATTHEW 21:2-3; LUKE 19:30-31

Go into the city, and a man carrying a jar of water will meet you; follow him, and wherever he enters, say to the owner of the house, "The Teacher asks, Where is my guest room where I may eat the Passover with my disciples?" He will show you a large room upstairs, furnished and ready. Make preparations for us there.

— MARK 14:13-15; MATTHEW 26:18; LUKE 22:10-12

[While preparing to wash Peter's feet:] You do not know now what I am doing, but later you will understand. . . . Unless I wash you, you have no share with me. . . . One who has bathed does not need to wash, except for the feet, but is entirely clean. And you are clean, though not all of you. . . . Not all of you are clean. . . .

Do you know what I have done to you? You call me Teacher and Lord — and you are right, for that is what I am. So if I, your Lord and Teacher, have washed your feet, you also ought to wash one another's feet. For I have set you an example, that you also should do as I have done to you. Very truly, I tell you, servants are not greater than their master, nor are messengers greater than the one who sent them. If you know these things, you are blessed if you do them. I am not speaking of all of you; I know whom I have chosen. But it is to fulfill the scripture, "The one who ate my bread has lifted his heel against me." I tell you this now, before it occurs, so that when it does occur, you may believe that I am he.

– JOHN 13:7-8, 10, 12-19

Now the Son of Man has been glorified, and God has been glorified in him. If God has been glorified in him, God will also glorify him in himself and will glorify him at once. Little children, I am with you only a little longer. You will look for me; and as I said to the Jews so now I say to you, "Where I am going, you cannot come."

– JOHN 13:31-33

Where I am going, you cannot follow me now; but you will follow afterward.

– JOHN 13:36

I have eagerly desired to eat this Passover with you

before I suffer; for I tell you, I will not eat it until it is fulfilled in the kingdom of God. — LUKE 22:15-16

Take, eat; this [bread] is my body.... Drink from it [a cup of wine], all of you; for this is my blood of the covenant, which is poured out for many for the forgiveness of sins. I tell you, I will never again drink of this fruit of the vine until that day when I drink it new with you in my Father's kingdom.
— MATTHEW 26:26-29; MARK 14:22-25; LUKE 22:17-18

This [bread] is my body, which is given for you. Do this in remembrance of me.
— LUKE 22:19; 1 CORINTHIANS 11:24

This cup is the new covenant in my blood. Do this, as often as you drink it, in remembrance of me. For as often as you eat this bread and drink the cup, you proclaim the Lord's death until he comes.
— 1 CORINTHIANS 11:25-26; LUKE 22:20

You will all become deserters because of me this night; for it is written,

"I will strike the shepherd, and the sheep of the flock will be scattered."

But after I am raised up, I will go ahead of you to Galilee. — MATTHEW 26:31-32; MARK 14:27-28

Truly I tell you, one of you will betray me, one who is eating with me.

— MARK 14:18; MATTHEW 26:21; JOHN 13:21

The one who has dipped his hand into the bowl with me will betray me. The Son of Man goes as it is written of him, but woe to that one by whom the Son of Man is betrayed! It would have been better for that one not to have been born.

— MATTHEW 26:23-24; MARK 14:20-21; LUKE 22:21-22; JOHN 13:26

[Judas, who betrayed him, said, "Surely not I, Rabbi?" He replied:] You have said so.

— MATTHEW 26:25; CF. MARK 14:19

Do quickly what you [Judas] are going to do.

— JOHN 13:27; CF. MATTHEW 26:50

Simon, Simon, listen! Satan has demanded to sift all of you like wheat, but I have prayed for you that your own faith may not fail; and you, when once you have turned back, strengthen your brothers.... I tell you, Peter, the cock will not crow this day, until you have denied three times that you know me.

— LUKE 22:31-32, 34, 61; MATTHEW 26:34; MARK 14:30; JOHN 13:38

Did I not choose you, the twelve? Yet one of you [Judas]

is a devil.                                    — John 6:70

[At Gethsemane:] Sit here while I go over there and pray.... I am deeply grieved, even to death; remain here, and stay awake with me.... My Father, if it is possible, let this cup pass from me; yet not what I want but what you want.... [To his three disciples:] So, could you not stay awake with me one hour? Stay awake and pray that you may not come into the time of trial; the spirit indeed is willing, but the flesh is weak.... My Father, if this cannot pass unless I drink it, your will be done.

— Matthew 26:36, 38-39, 40-42;
Mark 14:32, 34, 36-38, 41; Luke 22:40, 42, 46

Now my soul is troubled. And what should I say — "Father, save me from this hour"? No, it is for this reason that I have come to this hour. Father, glorify your name.                                    — John 12:27-28

Father, the hour has come; glorify your Son so that the Son may glorify you, since you have given him authority over all people, to give eternal life to all whom you have given him. And this is eternal life, that they may know you, the only true God, and Jesus Christ whom you have sent. I glorified you on earth by finishing the work that you gave me to do. So now, Father, glorify me in your own presence with the glory that I had in your presence before the world existed.    — JOHN 17:1-5

Are you [three disciples] still sleeping and taking your rest? Enough! The hour has come; the Son of Man is betrayed into the hands of sinners. Get up, let us be going. See, my betrayer is at hand.

— MARK 14:41-42; MATTHEW 26:45-46

When I sent you out without a purse, bag, or sandals, did you lack anything?... But now, the one who has a purse must take it, and likewise a bag. And the one who has no sword sell his cloak and buy one. For I tell you, this scripture must be fulfilled in me, "And he was counted among the lawless"; and indeed what is written about me is being fulfilled.    — LUKE 22:35-37

Judas, is it with a kiss that you are betraying the Son of Man?    — LUKE 22:48

Whom are you [Roman soldiers and Jewish temple police] looking for?... I am he.... Whom are you looking for?... I told you that I am he. So if you are looking for me, let these men [the disciples] go.

— JOHN 18:4-5, 7-8

Put your [Peter] sword back into its place; for all who take the sword will perish by the sword. Do you think that I cannot appeal to my Father, and he will at once send me more than twelve legions of angels? But how then would the scriptures be fulfilled, which say it must happen in this way?

– MATTHEW 26:52-54; CF. LUKE 22:51; JOHN 18:11

Have you come out with swords and clubs to arrest me as though I were a bandit? Day after day I sat in the temple teaching, and you did not arrest me. But all this has taken place, so that the scriptures of the prophets may be fulfilled.

– MATTHEW 26:55-56; MARK 14:48-49; LUKE 22:52-53

But this is your [chief priests, officers of the temple police, elders] hour, and the power of darkness!

– LUKE 22:53

I have spoken openly to the world; I have always taught in synagogues and in the temple, where all Jews come together. I have said nothing in secret. Why do you [the high priest] ask me [about my disciples and teachings]? Ask those who heard what I said to them; they know what I said. . . . If I have spoken wrongly, testify to the wrong. But if I have spoken rightly, why do you [one of the Jewish temple police] strike me?

– JOHN 18:20-21, 23

If I tell you [that I am the Christ], you will not believe;

and if I question you, you will not answer. But from now on the Son of Man will be seated at the right hand of the power of God.

— LUKE 22:67-69

I am [the Christ]; and

> "you [the high priest] will see the Son of Man
> seated at the right hand of the Power,"
> and "coming with the clouds of heaven."

— MARK 14:62; MATTHEW 26:64

You [Pilate] would have no power over me unless it had been given you from above; therefore the one [the high priest] who handed me over to you is guilty of a greater sin.

— JOHN 19:11

[From the cross:] Eli, Eli, lema sabachthani? [That is,] My God, my God, why have you forsaken me?

— MATTHEW 27:46; MARK 15:34

[From the cross:] I am thirsty.

— JOHN 19:28

[From the cross:] It is finished.

— JOHN 19:30

[From the cross:] Father, into your hands I commend my spirit.

— LUKE 23:46

[On the first day of the new week:] Woman [Mary], why

are you weeping? Whom are you looking for?...
Mary!...Do not hold on to me, because I [the risen
Christ] have not yet ascended to the Father. But go to
my brothers and say to them, "I am ascending to my
Father and your Father, to my God and your God."

– JOHN 20:15-17

Peace be with you....Why are you frightened, and why
do doubts arise in your hearts? Look at my hands and
my feet; see that it is I myself. Touch me and see; for a
ghost does not have flesh and bones as you see that I
have.
– LUKE 24:36, 38-40

Greetings!...Do not be afraid; go and tell my brothers
to go to Galilee; there they will see me.

– MATTHEW 28:9-10

What are you discussing with each other while you walk
along?...What things?...Oh, how foolish you are, and
how slow of heart to believe all that the prophets have
declared! Was it not necessary that the Christ should
suffer these things and then enter into his glory?

– LUKE 24:17, 19, 25-26

Very truly, I tell you, if you ask anything of the Father in
my name, he will give it to you. Until now you have not
asked for anything in my name. Ask and you will

receive, so that your joy may be complete.

— JOHN 16:23-24

Do not be afraid; I am the first and the last, and the living one. I was dead, and see, I am alive forever and ever; and I have the keys of Death and of Hades.

— REVELATION 1:17-18

See, I am coming soon; my reward is with me, to repay according to everyone's work. I am the Alpha and the Omega, the first and the last, the beginning and the end.

— REVELATION 22:12-13

These words are trustworthy and true, for the Lord, the God of the spirits of the prophets, has sent his angel to show his servants what must soon take place.

See, I am coming soon! Blessed is the one who keeps the words of the prophecy of this book.

— REVELATION 22:6-7

These are my words that I spoke to you while I was still with you — that everything written about me in the law of Moses, the prophets, and the psalms must be fulfilled.... Thus it is written, that the Christ is to suffer and to rise from the dead on the third day, and that repentance and forgiveness of sins is to be proclaimed in his name to all nations, beginning from Jerusalem. You are witnesses of these things. And see, I am sending upon you what my Father promised; so stay here in the city until you have been clothed with power from on high.

— LUKE 24:44, 46-49

# THE
# MESSAGE
# OF
# CHRIST

# LOVE

"You shall love the Lord your God with all your heart, and with all your soul, and with all your mind." This is the greatest and first commandment. And a second is like it: "You shall love your neighbor as yourself." On these two commandments hang all the law and the prophets.

— MATTHEW 22:37-40; MARK 12:29-31

By this evidence everyone will know that you are my disciples, if you have love for one another.

— JOHN 13:35

As the Father has loved me, so I have loved you; abide in my love. If you keep my commandments, you will abide in my love, just as I have kept my Father's

commandments and abide in his love. I have said these things to you so that my joy may be in you, and that your joy may be complete.
— JOHN 15:9-11

They who have my commandments and keep them are those who love me; and those who love me will be loved by my Father, and I will love them and reveal myself to them.
— JOHN 14:21

This is my commandment, that you love one another as I have loved you. No one has greater love than this, to lay down one's life for one's friends. You are my friends if you do what I command you. I do not call you servants any longer, because the servant does not know what the master is doing; but I have called you friends, because I have made known to you everything that I have heard from my Father.
— JOHN 15:12-15; 13:34

You have heard that it was said, "You shall love your neighbor and hate your enemy." But I say to you, Love your enemies and pray for those who persecute you, so that you may be children of your Father in heaven; for he makes his sun rise on the evil and on the good, and sends rain on the righteous and on the unrighteous.

— MATTHEW 5:43-45

If you love those who love you, what credit is that to

you? For even sinners love those who love them. If you do good to those who do good to you, what credit is that to you? For even sinners do the same. If you lend to those from whom you hope to receive, what credit is that to you? Even sinners lend to sinners, to receive as much again. But love your enemies, do good, and lend, expecting nothing in return. Your reward will be great, and you will be children of the Most High; for he is kind to the ungrateful and the wicked. Be merciful, just as your Father is merciful.

— LUKE 6:32-36; CF. 7:41-43; MATTHEW 5:46-47

Be perfect [in love to all], therefore, as your heavenly Father is perfect.

— MATTHEW 5:48

It is more blessed to give than to receive.

— ACTS 20:35

But I say to you that listen, Love your enemies, do good to those who hate you, bless those who curse you, pray for those who abuse you. If anyone strikes you on the cheek, offer the other also; and from anyone who takes away your coat do not withhold even your shirt. Give to everyone who begs from you; and if anyone takes away your goods, do not ask for them again. Do to others as you would have them do to you.

— LUKE 6:27-31

If God were your Father, you would love me, for I came

from God and now I am here. I did not come on my own, but he sent me. — JOHN 8:42; CF. 7:28-29

# LIGHT

---

I am the light of the world. Whoever follows me will never walk in darkness but will have the light of life.

– John 8:12

The light is with you for a little longer. Walk while you have the light, so that the darkness may not overtake you. If you walk in the darkness, you do not know where you are going. While you have the light, believe in the light, so that you may become children of light.

– John 12:35-36

Are there not twelve hours of daylight? Those who walk during the day do not stumble, because they see the light of this world. But those who walk at night stumble, because the light is not in them. — John 11:9-10

Neither this [blind] man nor his parents sinned; he was born blind so that God's works might be revealed in him. We must work the works of him who sent me while it is day; night is coming when no one can work. As long as I am in the world, I am the light of the world. . . . [Spreading mud on the man's eyes, he said:] Go, wash in the pool of Siloam. . . . Do you believe in the Son of Man? . . . You have seen him, and the one speaking with you is he. . . . I came into this world for judgment so that those who do not see may see, and those who do see may become blind.

— John 9:3-5, 7, 35, 37, 39

And this is the judgment, that the light has come into the world, and people loved darkness rather than light because their deeds were evil. For all who do evil hate the light and do not come to the light, so that their deeds may not be exposed. But those who do what is true come to the light, so that it may be clearly seen that their deeds have been done in God. — John 3:19-21

Your eye is the lamp of your body. If your eye is healthy, your whole body is full of light; but if it is not healthy, your body is full of darkness. Therefore consider whether the light in you is not darkness. If then your whole body is full of light, with no part of it in darkness, it will be as full of light as when a lamp gives you light with its rays.

– Luke 11:34-36; Matthew 6:22-23

You are the light of the world. A city built on a hill cannot be hid. No one after lighting a lamp puts it under the bushel basket, but on the lampstand, and it gives light to all in the house. In the same way, let your light shine before others, so that they may see your good works and give glory to your Father in heaven.

– Matthew 5:14-16; Mark 4:21; Luke 8:16, 11:33

For nothing is hidden that will not be disclosed, nor is anything secret that will not become known and come to light. Then pay attention to how you listen; for to those who have, more will be given; and from those who do not have, even what they seem to have will be taken away.

– Luke 8:17-18; Mark 4:22-23

Beware of the yeast of the Pharisees, that is, their hypocrisy. Nothing is covered up that will not be uncovered, and nothing secret that will not become known. Therefore whatever you have said in the dark will be heard in the light, and what you have whispered behind closed doors will be proclaimed from the housetops.

— LUKE 12:1-3; CF. MATTHEW 10:26-27

If you continue in my word, you are truly my disciples; and you will know the truth, and the truth will make you free.

— JOHN 8:31-32

You say that I am a king. For this I was born, and for this I came into the world, to testify to the truth. Everyone who belongs to the truth listens to my voice.

— JOHN 18:37

# FORGIVENESS

Receive the Holy Spirit. If you forgive the sins of any, they are forgiven them; if you retain the sins of any, they are retained.

– John 20:22-23

For if you forgive others their trespasses, your heavenly Father will also forgive you; but if you do not forgive others, neither will your Father forgive your trespasses.

– Matthew 6:14-15; Mark 11:25

If another member of the church sins against you, go and point out the fault when the two of you are alone. If the member listens to you, you have regained that one. But if you are not listened to, take one or two others along with you, so that every word may be confirmed by the evidence of two or three witnesses. If the member refuses to listen to them, tell it to the church; and if the offender refuses to listen even to the church, let such a one be to you as a Gentile and a tax collector.

– MATTHEW 18:15-17

Be on your guard! If another disciple sins, you must rebuke the offender, and if there is repentance, you must forgive. And if the same person sins against you seven times a day, and turns back to you seven times and says, "I repent," you must forgive.

– LUKE 17:3-4

[Peter came and said to him, "Lord, if another member of the church sins against me, how often should I forgive? As many as seven times?"] Not seven times, but, I tell you, seventy times seven.

– MATTHEW 18:22

So when you are offering your gift at the altar, if you remember that your brother or sister has something against you, leave your gift there before the altar and go; first be reconciled to your brother or sister, and then come and offer your gift.

– MATTHEW 5:23-24

Come to terms quickly with your accuser while you are on the way to court with him, or your accuser may hand you over to the judge, and the judge to the guard, and you will be thrown into prison. Truly I tell you, you will never get out until you have paid the last penny.

— MATTHEW 5:25-26; LUKE 12:58-59

For this reason the kingdom of heaven may be compared to a king who wished to settle accounts with his slaves. When he began the reckoning, one who owed him ten thousand talents was brought to him; and, as he could not pay, his lord ordered him to be sold, together with his wife and children and all his possessions, and payment to be made. So the slave fell on his knees before him, saying, "Have patience with me, and I will pay you everything." And out of pity for him, the lord of that slave released him and forgave him the debt. But that same slave, as he went out, came upon one of his fellow slaves who owed him a hundred denarii; and seizing him by the throat, he said, "Pay what you owe." Then his fellow slave fell down and pleaded with him, "Have patience with me, and I will pay you." But he refused; then he went and threw him into prison until he would pay the debt. When his fellow slaves saw what had happened, they were greatly distressed, and they went and reported to their lord all that had taken place. Then his lord summoned him and said to him, "You wicked slave! I forgave you all that debt because you pleaded with me. Should you not have had mercy on your fellow slave, as I had mercy on you?" And in anger his lord handed him over to be tortured until he would pay his entire debt. So my heavenly Father will also do to every one of you, if you do not forgive your brother or sister from your heart. — MATTHEW 18:23-35

Do you see this woman? I entered your [Simon's] house; you gave me no water for my feet, but she has bathed my feet with her tears and dried them with her hair. You gave me no kiss, but from the time I came in she has not stopped kissing my feet. You did not anoint my head with oil, but she has anointed my feet with ointment. Therefore, I tell you, her sins, which were many, have been forgiven; hence she has shown great love. But the one to whom little is forgiven, loves little.... Your sins are forgiven.... Your faith has saved you; go in peace.

— LUKE 7:44-48, 50

Do not judge, and you will not be judged; do not condemn, and you will not be condemned. Forgive, and you will be forgiven; give, and it will be given to you.

— LUKE 6:37-38; MATTHEW 7:1-2

Let anyone among you who is without sin be the first to throw a stone at her [an adulteress].... Woman, where are they? Has no one condemned you?... Neither do I condemn you. Go your way, and from now on do not sin again.

– JOHN 8:7, 10-11

There was a man who had two sons. The younger of them said to his father, "Father, give me the share of the property that will belong to me." So he divided his property between them. A few days later the younger son gathered all he had and traveled to a distant country, and there he squandered his property in dissolute living. When he had spent everything, a severe famine took place throughout that country, and he began to be in need. So he went and hired himself out to one of the citizens of that country, who sent him to his fields to feed the pigs. He would gladly have filled himself with the pods that the pigs were eating; and no one gave him anything. But when he came to himself he said, "How many of my father's hired hands have bread enough and to spare, but here I am dying of hunger! I will get up and go to my father, and I will say to him, 'Father, I have sinned against heaven and before you; I am no longer worthy to be called your son; treat me like one of your hired hands.'" So he set off and went to his father. But while he was still far off, his father saw him and was filled with compassion; he ran and put his arms around him and kissed him. Then the son said to him, "Father, I have sinned against heaven and before you; I am no longer worthy to be called your son." But the father said to his slaves, "Quickly, bring out a robe — the best one — and put it on him; put a ring on his finger and sandals on his feet. And get the fatted calf and kill it, and let us eat and celebrate; for this son of mine was dead and is alive again; he was lost and is found!" And they began to celebrate.

Now his elder son was in the field; and when he came and approached the house, he heard music and dancing. He called one of the slaves and asked what was going on. He replied, "Your brother has come, and your father has killed the fatted calf, because he has got him back safe and sound." Then he became angry and refused to go in. His father came out and began to plead with him. But he answered his father, "Listen! For all these years I have been working like a slave for you, and I have never disobeyed your command; yet you have never given me even a young goat so that I might celebrate with my friends. But when this son of yours came back, who has devoured your property with prostitutes, you killed the fatted calf for him!" Then the father said to him, "Son, you are always with me, and all that is mine is yours. But we had to celebrate and rejoice, because this brother of yours was dead and has come to life; he was lost and has been found."

– LUKE 15:11-32

Which one of you, having a hundred sheep and losing one of them, does not leave the ninety-nine in the wilderness and go after the one that is lost until he finds it? When he has found it, he lays it on his shoulders and rejoices. And when he comes home, he calls together his friends and neighbors, saying to them, "Rejoice with me, for I have found my sheep that was lost." Just so, I tell you, there will be more joy in heaven over one sinner who repents than over ninety-nine righteous persons who need no repentance.

– LUKE 15:4-7; CF. 8-10; MATTHEW 18:12-13

So it is not the will of your Father in heaven that one of these little ones [disciples] should be lost.

– MATTHEW 18:14

Do you [a man ill for thirty-eight years] want to be made well? . . . Stand up, take your mat and walk. . . . See, you have been made well! Do not sin any more, so that nothing worse happens to you.

– JOHN 5:6, 8, 14

Take heart, son [a paralytic]; your sins are forgiven.

– MATTHEW 9:2; MARK 2:5; LUKE 5:20

Why do you think evil in your hearts? For which is easier, to say, "Your sins are forgiven," or to say, "Stand up and walk"? But so that you may know that the Son of

Man has authority on earth to forgive sins [he then said to the paralytic:] Stand up, take your bed and go to your home.
— MATTHEW 9:4-6; LUKE 5:22-24; MARK 2:8-11

Truly I tell you [repentant thief on the cross next to him], today you will be with me in Paradise.
— LUKE 23:43

[From the cross:] Father, forgive them; for they do not know what they are doing.
— LUKE 23:34

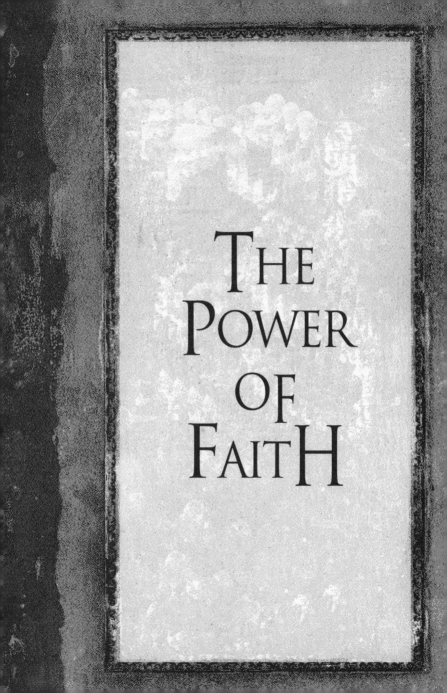

THE
POWER
OF
FAITH

# THE POWER
## OF
## FAITH

H ave faith in God. Truly I tell you, if you say to this mountain, "Be taken up and thrown into the sea," and if you do not doubt in your heart, but believe that what you say will come to pass, it will be done for you. So I tell you, whatever you ask for in prayer, believe that you have received it, and it will be yours.

— MARK 11:22-24; MATTHEW 21:21-22; CF. LUKE 17:6

For truly I tell you, if you have faith the size of a mustard seed, you will say to this mountain, "Move from here to there," and it will move; and nothing will be impossible for you. — MATTHEW 17:20-21

Let anyone who is thirsty come to me, and let the one who believes in me drink. As the scripture has said,

"Out of the believer's heart shall flow rivers of living water."

— JOHN 7:37-38

Ask, and it will be given you; search, and you will find; knock, and the door will be opened for you. For everyone who asks receives, and everyone who searches finds, and for everyone who knocks, the door will be opened.

— MATTHEW 7:7-8; LUKE 11:9-10

Put out into the deep water and let down your nets for a catch.... Do not be afraid; from now on you will be catching people.

— LUKE 5:4, 10

Children [disciples], you have no fish, have you?... Cast the net to the right side of the boat, and you will find some.... Bring some of the fish that you have just caught.... Come and have breakfast.

— JOHN 21:5-6, 10, 12

Go; let it be done for you [the curing of a centurion's paralyzed servant] according to your faith.

— MATTHEW 8:13; CF. 8:7; LUKE 7:9

[To two blind men:] Do you believe that I am able to do this?... According to your faith let it be done to you. [And their eyes were opened.]

— MATTHEW 9:28-29; CF. 20:32

[To a Canaanite whose daughter is demon possessed:] Woman, great is your faith! Let it be done for you as you wish. [And her daughter was healed instantly.]

– Matthew 15:28

[To someone crippled by a spirit for eighteen years:] Woman, you are set free from your ailment.

– Luke 13:12

Who touched me?... Someone touched me; for I noticed that power had gone out from me.... Daughter [who had been suffering from hemorrhages for twelve years], your faith has made you well; go in peace.

– Luke 8:45-46, 48; Mark 5:30, 34; Matthew 9:22

[To Bartimaeus, a blind beggar:] What do you want me to do for you?... Receive your sight; your faith has saved you. – Luke 18:41-42; Mark 10:51-52; cf. 8:23, 26

Ephphatha. [That is,] Be opened [the ears of a deaf man].

– Mark 7:34

[To ten lepers seeking to be made well:] Go and show yourselves to the priests.... [Then one of them, when he saw that he was healed, turned back, praising God with a loud voice.] Were not ten made clean? But the other nine, where are they? Was none of them found to return and give praise to God except this foreigner?... Get up and go on your way; your faith has made you well.

— LUKE 17:14, 17-19

This illness [of Lazarus] does not lead to death; rather it is for God's glory, so that the Son of God may be glorified through it.... Our friend Lazarus has fallen asleep, but I am going there to awaken him.... Lazarus is dead. For your [the disciples'] sake I am glad that I was not there, so that you may believe. But let us go to him [at his tomb].... Your [Martha's] brother will rise again.... I am the resurrection and the life. Those who believe in me, even though they die, will live, and everyone who lives and believes in me will never die. Do you believe this?... Where have you [Mary] laid him?... Take away the stone.... Did I not tell you [Martha] that if you believed, you would see the glory of God?... Father, I thank you for having heard me. I knew that you always hear me, but I have said this for the sake of the crowd standing here, so that they may believe that you sent me.... Lazarus, come out!... Unbind him, and let him go.

— JOHN 11:4, 11, 14-15, 23, 25-26, 34, 39, 40-44

[To a mother:] Do not weep.... [To her dead son:] Young man, I say to you, rise! [The dead man sat up and began to speak.]

— LUKE 7:13-14

[To a ruler regarding his dead daughter:] Do not fear. Only believe, and she will be saved. . . . Do not weep; for she is not dead but sleeping. . . . Child, get up!  [Her spirit returned, and she got up at once.]

    – LUKE 8:50, 52, 54; MARK 5:36, 39, 41; MATTHEW 9:24

[To a royal official whose son lay ill:] Unless you see signs and wonders you will not believe. . . . Go; your son will live.

    – JOHN 4:48, 50, 53

You faithless generation, how much longer must I be among you?  How much longer must I put up with you? Bring him [a man's son possessed from childhood] to me. . . . How long has this been happening to him? . . . All things can be done for the one who believes. . . . You spirit that keeps this boy from speaking and hearing, I command you, come out of him, and never enter him again! . . . This kind [of spirit] can come out only through prayer.

    – MARK 9:19, 21, 23, 25, 29;
    MATTHEW 17:17, 20; LUKE 9:41

Let us go across to the other side [of the sea of Galilee]. . . . [A great windstorm arose.]  Peace!  Be still! [Then the wind ceased, and there was a dead calm.] . . . Why are you afraid?  Have you still no faith?

    – MARK 4:35, 39-40; LUKE 8:22, 25; MATTHEW 8:26

[While walking toward the disciples on the sea:] Take heart, it is I; do not be afraid.

— MATTHEW 14:27; MARK 6:50; JOHN 6:20

[To Peter, who tried to walk on the water but grew frightened and began to sink:] You of little faith, why did you doubt?

— MATTHEW 14:31

[To the disciple Thomas:] Put your finger here and see my hands. Reach out your hand and put it in my side. Do not doubt but believe.... Have you believed because you have seen me? Blessed are those who have not seen and yet have come to believe.

— JOHN 20:27, 29

In a certain city there was a judge who neither feared God nor had respect for people. In that city there was a widow who kept coming to him and saying, "Grant me justice against my opponent." For a while he refused; but later he said to himself, "Though I have no fear of God and no respect for anyone, yet because this widow keeps bothering me, I will grant her justice, so that she may not wear me out by continually coming." ... Listen to what the unjust judge says. And will not God grant justice to his chosen ones who cry to him day and night? Will he delay long in helping them? I tell you, he will quickly grant justice to them. And yet, when the Son of Man comes, will he find faith on earth?

— LUKE 18:2-8

[To Nicodemus:] Are you a teacher of Israel, and yet you do not understand these things?

Very truly, I tell you, we speak of what we know and testify to what we have seen; yet you do not receive our testimony. If I have told you about earthly things and you do not believe, how can you believe if I tell you about heavenly things? No one has ascended into heaven except the one who descended from heaven, the Son of Man. And just as Moses lifted up the serpent in the wilderness, so must the Son of Man be lifted up, that whoever believes in him may have eternal life.

– John 3:10-15

Therefore I tell you, do not worry about your life, what you will eat, or about your body, what you will wear. For life is more than food, and the body more than clothing. Consider the ravens: they neither sow nor reap, they have neither storehouse nor barn, and yet God feeds them. Of how much more value are you than the birds! And can any of you by worrying add a single hour to your span of life? If then you are not able to do so small a thing as that, why do you worry about the rest? Consider the lilies, how they grow: they neither toil nor spin; yet I tell you, even Solomon in all his glory was not clothed like one of these. But if God so clothes the grass of the field, which is alive today and tomorrow is thrown into the oven, how much more will he clothe you — you of little faith!  And do not keep striving for what you are to eat and what you are to drink, and do not keep worrying. For it is the nations of the world that strive after these things, and your Father knows that you need them.  Instead, strive for his kingdom, and these things will be given to you as well.

– LUKE 12:22-31; MATTHEW 6:25-33

So do not worry about tomorrow, for tomorrow will bring worries of its own.  Today's trouble is enough for today.

– MATTHEW 6:34

This is the work of God, that you believe in him whom he has sent.

– JOHN 6:29

What is impossible for mortals is possible for God.

– LUKE 18:27; MATTHEW 19:26; MARK 10:2

# THE
# KINGDOM
# OF
# HEAVEN

# The Nature of The Kingdom

My kingdom is not from this world.

— John 18:36

The kingdom of God is not coming with things that can be observed; nor will they say, "Look, here it is!" or "There it is!" For, in fact, the kingdom of God is among you.

— Luke 17:20-21

For the kingdom of heaven is like a landowner who went out early in the morning to hire laborers for his vineyard. After agreeing with the laborers for the usual daily wage [a denarius], he sent them into his vineyard. When he went out about nine o'clock, he saw others standing idle in the marketplace; and he said to them, "You also go into the vineyard, and I will pay you whatever is right." So they went. When he went out again about noon and about three o'clock, he did the same. And about five o'clock he went out and found others standing around; and he said to them, "Why are you standing here idle all day?" They said to him, "Because no one has hired us." He said to them, "You also go into the vineyard." When evening came, the owner of the vineyard said to his manager, "Call the laborers and give them their pay, beginning with the last and then going to the first." When those hired about five o'clock came, each of them received the usual daily wage. Now when the first came, they thought they would receive more; but each of them also received the usual daily wage. And when they received it, they grumbled against the landowner, saying, "These last worked only one hour, and you have made them equal to us who have borne the burden of the day and the scorching heat." But he replied to one of them, "Friend, I am doing you no wrong; did you not agree with me for the usual daily wage? Take what belongs to you and go; I choose to give to this last the same as I give to you. Am I not allowed to do what I choose with what belongs to me? Or are you envious because I am generous?" So the last will be first, and the first will be last.

— MATTHEW 20:1-16

Truly I tell you, there is no one who has left house or brothers or sisters or mother or father or children or fields, for my sake and for the sake of the good news, who will not receive a hundredfold now in this age... and in the age to come eternal life. But many who are first will be last, and the last will be first.

— MARK 10:29-31; LUKE 18:29-30; MATTHEW 19:29-30

Truly I tell you, at the renewal of all things, when the Son of Man is seated on the throne of his glory, you who have followed me will also sit on twelve thrones, judging the twelve tribes of Israel.

— MATTHEW 19:28

The kingdom of God is as if someone would scatter seed on the ground, and would sleep and rise night and day, and the seed would sprout and grow, he does not know how. The earth produces of itself, first the stalk, then the head, then the full grain in the head. But when the grain is ripe, at once he puts in with his sickle, because the harvest has come.

— MARK 4:26-29

The kingdom of heaven may be compared to someone who sowed good seed in his field; but while everybody was asleep, an enemy came and sowed weeds among the wheat, and then went away. So when the plants came up and bore grain, then the weeds appeared as well. And the slaves of the householder came and said to him, "Master, did you not sow good seed in your field? Where, then, did these weeds come from?" He answered, "An enemy has done this." The slaves said to him, "Then do you want us to go and gather them?" But he replied, "No; for in gathering the weeds you would uproot the wheat along with them. Let both of them grow together until the harvest; and at harvest time I will tell the reapers, Collect the weeds first and bind them in bundles to be burned, but gather the wheat into my barn." . . . The one who sows the good seed is the Son of Man; the field is the world, and the good seed are the children of the kingdom; the weeds are the children of the evil one, and the enemy who sowed them is the devil; the harvest is at the end of the age, and the reapers are angels. Just as the weeds are collected and burned up with fire, so will it be at the end of the age. The Son of Man will send his angels, and they will collect out of his kingdom all causes of sin and all evildoers, and they will throw them into the furnace of fire, where there will be weeping and gnashing of teeth. Then the righteous will shine like the sun in the kingdom of their Father. Let anyone with ears listen!

– MATTHEW 13:24-30, 37-43

The kingdom of heaven is like a mustard seed that someone took and sowed in his field; it is the smallest of all the seeds, but when it has grown it is the greatest of shrubs and becomes a tree, so that the birds of the air come and make nests in its branches.

– Matthew 13:31-32; Mark 4:31-32; Luke 13:19

The kingdom of heaven is like treasure hidden in a field, which someone found and hid; then in his joy he goes and sells all that he has and buys that field.

– Matthew 13:44

Again, the kingdom of heaven is like a merchant in search of fine pearls; on finding one pearl of great value, he went and sold all that he had and bought it.

– Matthew 13:45-46

Again, the kingdom of heaven is like a net that was thrown into the sea and caught fish of every kind; when it was full, they drew it ashore, sat down, and put the good into baskets but threw out the bad. So it will be at the end of the age. The angels will come out and separate the evil from the righteous and throw them into the furnace of fire, where there will be weeping and gnashing of teeth.

– Matthew 13:47-50

Therefore every scribe who has been trained for the

kingdom of heaven is like the master of a household who brings out of his treasure what is new and what is old.

— MATTHEW 13:52

Then the kingdom of heaven will be like this. Ten bridesmaids [virgins] took their lamps and went to meet the bridegroom. Five of them were foolish, and five were wise. When the foolish took their lamps, they took no oil with them; but the wise took flasks of oil with their lamps. As the bridegroom was delayed, all of them became drowsy and slept. But at midnight there was a shout, "Look! Here is the bridegroom! Come out to meet him." Then all those bridesmaids got up and trimmed their lamps. The foolish said to the wise, "Give us some of your oil, for our lamps are going out." But the wise replied, "No! there will not be enough for you and for us; you had better go to the dealers and buy some for yourselves." And while they went to buy it, the bridegroom came, and those who were ready went with him into the wedding banquet; and the door was shut. Later the other bridesmaids came also, saying, "Lord, lord, open to us." But he replied, "Truly I tell you, I do not know you." Keep awake therefore, for you know neither the day nor the hour.

— MATTHEW 25:1-13

Blessed are the poor in spirit, for theirs is the kingdom

of heaven.

– MATTHEW 5:3; LUKE 6:20

Blessed are those who mourn, for they will be comforted.

– MATTHEW 5:4

Blessed are you who weep now, for you will laugh.

– LUKE 6:21

Blessed are the meek, for they will inherit the earth.

– MATTHEW 5:5

Blessed are those who hunger and thirst for righteousness, for they will be filled.

– MATTHEW 5:6; LUKE 6:21

Blessed are the merciful, for they will receive mercy.

– MATTHEW 5:7

Blessed are the pure in heart, for they will see God.

– MATTHEW 5:8

Blessed are the peacemakers, for they will be called children of God.

– MATTHEW 5:9

Blessed are those who are persecuted for righteousness' sake, for theirs is the kingdom of heaven.

– MATTHEW 5:10

Blessed are you when people revile you and persecute you and utter all kinds of evil against you falsely on my account. Rejoice and be glad, for your reward is great in heaven, for in the same way they persecuted the prophets who were before you.

— MATTHEW 5:11-12; LUKE 6:22-23

You are not far from the kingdom of God.

— MARK 12:34

# TO ENTER THE KINGDOM

Repent, for the kingdom of heaven is at hand.

— MATTHEW 4:17

Very truly, I tell you, no one can see the kingdom of God without being born from above [anew]. . . . Very truly, I tell you, no one can enter the kingdom of God without being born of water and Spirit. What is born of the flesh is flesh, and what is born of the Spirit is spirit. Do not be astonished that I said to you, "You must be born from above." The wind blows where it chooses, and you hear the sound of it, but you do not know where it comes from or where it goes. So it is with everyone who is born of the Spirit.

— JOHN 3:3, 5-8

Do not be afraid, little flock, for it is your Father's good pleasure to give you the kingdom.

— LUKE 12:32

Everyone therefore who acknowledges me before others, I also will acknowledge before my Father in heaven; but whoever denies me before others, I also will deny before my Father in heaven.

— MATTHEW 10:32-33; LUKE 12:8-9

A nobleman went to a distant country to get royal power for himself and then return. He summoned ten of his slaves, and gave them ten pounds [one pound: three months' wages], and said to them, "Do business with these until I come back." But the citizens of his country hated him and sent a delegation after him. saying, "We do not want this man to rule over us." When he returned, having received royal power, he ordered these slaves, to whom he had given the money, to be summoned so that he might find out what they had gained by trading. The first came forward and said, "Lord, your pound has made ten more pounds." He said to him, "Well done, good slave! Because you have been trustworthy in a very small thing, take charge of ten cities." Then the second came, saying, "Lord, your pound has made five pounds." He said to him, "And you, rule over five cities." Then the other came, saying, "Lord, here is your pound. I wrapped it up in a piece of cloth, for I was afraid of you, because you are a harsh man; you take what you did not deposit, and reap what you did not sow." He said to him, "I will judge you by your own words, you wicked slave! You knew, did you, that I was a harsh man, taking what I did not deposit and reaping what I did not sow? Why then did you not put my money into the bank? Then when I returned, I could have collected it with interest." He said to the bystanders, "Take the pound from him and give it to the one who has the ten pounds." [And they said to him, "Lord, he has ten pounds!"] "I tell you, to all those who have, more will be given; but from those who have nothing, even what they have will be taken away. But as for these enemies of mine who did not want me to be king over them — bring them here and slaughter them in my presence."

– LUKE 19:12-27; CF. MATTHEW 13:12; 25:14-30

When the Son of Man comes in his glory, and all the angels with him, then he will sit on the throne of his glory. All the nations will be gathered before him, and he will separate people one from another as a shepherd separates the sheep from the goats, and he will put the sheep at his right hand and the goats at the left. Then the king will say to those at his right hand, "Come, you that are blessed by my Father, inherit the kingdom prepared for you from the foundation of the world; for I was hungry and you gave me food, I was thirsty and you gave me something to drink, I was a stranger and you welcomed me, I was naked and you gave me clothing, I was sick and you took care of me, I was in prison and you visited me." Then the righteous will answer him, "Lord, when was it that we saw you hungry and gave you food, or thirsty and gave you something to drink? And when was it that we saw you a stranger and welcomed you, or naked and gave you clothing? And when was it that we saw you sick or in prison and visited you?" And the king will answer them, "Truly I tell you, just as you did it to one of the least of these who are members of my family, you did it to me." Then he will say to those at his left hand, "You that are accursed, depart from me into the eternal fire prepared for the devil and his angels; for I was hungry and you gave me no food, I was thirsty and you gave me nothing to drink, I was a stranger and you did not welcome me, naked and you did not give me clothing, sick and in prison and you did not visit me." Then they also will answer, "Lord, when was it that we saw you hungry or thirsty or a stranger or naked or sick or in prison, and did not take care of you?" Then he will answer them, "Truly I tell you, just as you did not do it to one of the least of these, you did not do it to me." And these will go away into eternal punishment, but the righteous into eternal life.

— MATTHEW 25:31-46

Who then is the faithful and prudent manager whom his master will put in charge of his slaves, to give them their allowance of food at the proper time? Blessed is that slave whom his master will find at work when he arrives. Truly I tell you, he will put that one in charge of all his possessions. But if that slave says to himself, "My master is delayed in coming," and if he begins to beat the other slaves, men and women, and to eat and drink and get drunk, the master of that slave will come on a day when he does not expect him and at an hour that he does not know, and will cut him in pieces [cut him off], and put him with the unfaithful. That slave who knew what his master wanted, but did not prepare himself or do what was wanted, will receive a severe beating. But the one who did not know and did what deserved a beating will receive a light beating. From everyone to whom much has been given, much will be required; and from the one to whom much has been entrusted, even more will be demanded.

— LUKE 12:42-48; MATTHEW 24:45-51

Not everyone who says to me, "Lord, Lord," will enter the kingdom of heaven, but only the one who does the will of my Father in heaven. On that day many will say to me, "Lord, Lord, did we not prophesy in your name, and cast out demons in your name, and do many deeds of power in your name?" Then I will declare to them, "I never knew you; go away from me, you evildoers."

— MATTHEW 7:21-23

For I tell you, unless your righteousness exceeds that of the scribes and Pharisees, you will never enter the kingdom of heaven.

— MATTHEW 5:20

Therefore, whoever breaks [annuls] one of the least of these commandments, and teaches others to do the same, will be called least in the kingdom of heaven; but whoever does them and teaches them will be called great in the kingdom of heaven.

— MATTHEW 5:19

Enter through the narrow gate; for the gate is wide and the road is easy that leads to destruction, and there are many who take it. For the gate is narrow and the road is hard that leads to life, and there are few who find it.

— MATTHEW 7:13-14

Strive to enter through the narrow door; for many, I tell you, will try to enter and will not be able. When once the owner of the house has got up and shut the door, and you begin to stand outside and to knock at the door, saying, "Lord, open to us," then in reply he will say to you, "I do not know where you come from." Then you will begin to say, "We ate and drank with you, and you taught in our streets." But he will say, "I do not know where you come from; go away from me, all you evil-doers!" There will be weeping and gnashing of teeth when you see Abraham and Isaac and Jacob and all the prophets in the kingdom of God, and you yourselves thrown out. Then people will come from east and west, from north and south, and will eat in the kingdom of God. Indeed, some are last who will be first, and some are first who will be last.

– LUKE 13:24-30; MATTHEW 8:11-12; CF. 7:21-23

The kingdom of heaven may be compared to a king who gave a wedding banquet for his son. He sent his slaves to call those who had been invited to the wedding banquet, but they would not come. Again he sent other slaves, saying, "Tell those who have been invited: Look, I have prepared my dinner, my oxen and my fat calves have been slaughtered, and everything is ready; come to the wedding banquet." But they made light of it and went away, one to his farm, another to his business, while the rest seized his slaves, mistreated them, and killed them. The king was enraged. He sent his troops, destroyed those murderers, and burned their city. Then he said to his slaves, "The wedding is ready, but those invited were not worthy. Go therefore into the main streets, and invite everyone you find to the wedding banquet." Those slaves went out into the streets and gathered all whom they found, both good and bad; so the wedding hall was filled with guests.

But when the king came in to see the guests, he noticed a man there who was not wearing a wedding robe, and he said to him, "Friend, how did you get in here without a wedding robe?" And he was speechless. Then the king said to the attendants, "Bind him hand and foot, and throw him into the outer darkness, where there will be weeping and gnashing of teeth." For many are called, but few are chosen.

— MATTHEW 22:2-14; CF. LUKE 14:16-24

Whoever welcomes a prophet in the name of a prophet will receive a prophet's reward; and whoever welcomes a righteous person in the name of a righteous person will receive the reward of the righteous; and whoever gives even a cup of cold water to one of these little ones [disciples] in the name of a disciple — truly I tell you, none of these will lose their reward.

— MATTHEW 10:41-42

Those who find their life will lose it, and those who lose

their life for my sake will find it.

— MATTHEW 10:39

Do not store up for yourselves treasures on earth, where moth and rust consume and where thieves break in and steal; but store up for yourselves treasures in heaven, where neither moth nor rust consumes and where thieves do not break in and steal. For where your treasure is, there your heart will be also.

— MATTHEW 6:19-21; CF. LUKE 12:33-34

Do not work for the food that perishes, but for the food that endures for eternal life, which the Son of Man will give you. For it is on him that God the Father has set his seal.

— JOHN 6:27

Why do you ask me about what is good? There is only one who is good. If you wish to enter into life, keep the commandments.

— MATTHEW 19:17; CF. MARK 10:18; LUKE 18:19

[To the rich man desiring eternal life:] You know the commandments: "You shall not murder; You shall not commit adultery; You shall not steal; You shall not bear false witness; You shall not defraud; Honor your father and mother." . . . You lack one thing; go, sell what you own, and give [the money] to the poor, and you will have treasure in heaven; then come, follow me.

— MARK 10:19, 21; LUKE 18:20, 22; MATTHEW 19:18-19, 21

If any want to become my followers, let them deny themselves and take up their cross and follow me. For those who want to save their life will lose it, and those who lose their life for my sake, and the sake of the gospel, will save it. For what will it profit them to gain the whole world and forfeit their life? Indeed, what can they give in return for their life? Those who are ashamed of me and of my words in this adulterous and sinful generation, of them the Son of Man will also be ashamed when he comes in the glory of his Father with the holy angels.

— MARK 8:34-38; MATTHEW 16:24-27; LUKE 9:23-26

What do you think? A man had two sons; he went to the first and said, "Son, go and work in the vineyard today." He answered, "I will not"; but later he changed his mind and went. The father went to the second and said the same; and he answered, "I go, sir"; but he did not go. Which of the two did the will of his father? [The chief priests and elders said, "The first."] Truly I tell you, the tax collectors and the prostitutes are going into the king-dom of God ahead of you. For John [the Baptist] came to you in the way of righteousness and you did not believe him, but the tax collectors and the prostitutes believed him; and even after you saw it, you did not change your minds and believe him.

– MATTHEW 21:28-32

[Regarding Galileans who had been slain by Pilate's order while sacrificing in the temple:] Do you think that because these Galileans suffered in this way they were worse sinners than all other Galileans? No, I tell you; but unless you repent, you will all perish as they did. Or those eighteen who were killed when the tower of Siloam fell on them — do you think that they were worse offenders than all the others living in Jerusalem? No, I tell you; but unless you repent, you will all perish just as they did.

– LUKE 13:2-5

Listen! A sower went out to sow. And as he sowed, some seed fell on the path, and the birds came and ate it up. Other seed fell on rocky ground, where it did not have much soil, and it sprang up quickly, since it had no depth of soil. And when the sun rose, it was scorched; and since it had no root, it withered away. Other seed fell among thorns, and the thorns grew up and choked it, and it yielded no grain. Other seed fell into good soil and brought forth grain, growing up and increasing and yielding thirty and sixty and a hundredfold. . . . Let anyone with ears to hear listen!

— MARK 4:3-9; LUKE 8:5-8; MATTHEW 13:3-9

Do you not understand this parable? Then how will you understand all the parables? The sower sows the word. These are the ones on the path where the word is sown: when they hear, Satan immediately comes and takes away the word that is sown in them. And these are the ones sown on rocky ground: when they hear the word, they immediately receive it with joy. But they have no root, and endure only for a while; then, when trouble or persecution arises on account of the word, immediately they fall away [stumble]. And others are those sown among the thorns: those are the ones who hear the word, but the cares of the world, and the lure of wealth, and the desire for other things come in and choke the word, and it yields nothing. And these are the ones sown on the good soil: they hear the word and accept it and bear fruit, thirty and sixty and a hundredfold.

— MARK 4:13-20; LUKE 8:11-15; MATTHEW 13:18-23

To you it has been given to know the secrets of the kingdom of heaven, but to them [hostile listeners] it has not been given. For to those who have, more will be given, and they will have an abundance; but from those who have nothing, even what they have will be taken away. The reason I speak to them in parables is that "seeing they do not perceive, and hearing they do not listen, nor do they understand." With them indeed is fulfilled the prophecy of Isaiah that says:

> "You will indeed listen, but never understand,
>      you will indeed look, but never perceive.
> For this people's heart has grown dull,
>      and their ears are hard of hearing,
>           and they have shut their eyes;
> so that they might not look with their eyes,
>      and listen with their ears,
> and understand with their heart and turn —
>      and I would heal them."

But blessed are your eyes, for they see, and your ears, for they hear. Truly I tell you, many prophets and righteous people longed to see what you see, but did not see it, and to hear what you hear, but did not hear it.

– MATTHEW 13:11-17; MARK 4:11-12, 25;
LUKE 8:10, 10:23-24

There was a rich man who was dressed in purple and fine linen and who feasted sumptuously every day. And at his gate lay a poor man named Lazarus, covered with sores, who longed to satisfy his hunger with what fell from the rich man's table; even the dogs would come and lick his sores. The poor man died and was carried away by the angels to be with Abraham. The rich man also died and was buried. In Hades, where he was being tormented, he looked up and saw Abraham far away with Lazarus by his side. He called out, "Father Abraham, have mercy on me, and send Lazarus to dip the tip of his finger in water and cool my tongue; for I am in agony in these flames." But Abraham said, "Child, remember that during your lifetime you received your good things, and Lazarus in like manner evil things; but now he is comforted here, and you are in agony. Besides all this, between you and us a great chasm has been fixed, so that those who might want to pass from here to you cannot do so, and no one can cross from there to us." He said, "Then, father, I beg you to send him to my father's house — for I have five brothers — that he may warn them, so that they will not also come into this place of torment." Abraham said, "They have Moses and the prophets; they should listen to them." He said, "No, father Abraham; but if someone goes to them from the dead, they will repent." He said to him, "If they do not listen to Moses and the prophets, neither will they be convinced even if someone rises from the dead."

– LUKE 16:19-31

Truly I tell you, unless you change and become like children, you will never enter the kingdom of heaven. Whoever becomes humble like this child is the greatest in the kingdom of heaven. Whoever welcomes one such child in my name welcomes me.

— MATTHEW 18:3-5

Let the little children come to me; do not stop them; for it is to such as these that the kingdom of God belongs. Truly I tell you, whoever does not receive the kingdom of God as a little child will never enter it.

— MARK 10:14-15; LUKE 18:16-17; MATTHEW 19:14

The time is fulfilled, and the kingdom of God is at hand; repent, and believe in the good news.

— MARK 1:15

# WORDS
# OF
# WARNING

# THE WAGES
## OF SIN

Why do you call me "Lord, Lord," and do not do what I tell you?

— LUKE 6:46

Very truly, I tell you, everyone who commits sin is a slave to sin. The slave does not have a permanent place in the household; the son has a place there forever. So if the Son makes you free, you will be free indeed. I know that you are descendants of Abraham; yet you look for an opportunity to kill me, because there is no place in you for my word. I declare what I have seen in the Father's presence; as for you, you should do what you have heard from the Father.

— JOHN 8:34-38

I am going away, and you will search for me, but you

will die in your sin. Where I am going, you cannot come....You are from below, I am from above; you are of this world, I am not of this world. I told you that you would die in your sins, for you will die in your sins unless you believe that I am he.     – JOHN 8:21, 23-25

And why do you break the commandment of God for the sake of your tradition? For God said, "Honor your father and your mother," and, "Whoever speaks evil of father or mother must surely die." But you say that whoever tells his father or his mother, "Whatever support you might have had from me is given to God," then that person need not honor the father [or the mother]. So, for the sake of your tradition, you make void the word of God. You hypocrites! Isaiah prophesied rightly about you when he said:

> "This people honors me with their lips,
>     but their hearts are far from me;
>  in vain do they worship me,
>      teaching human precepts as doctrines."
> – MATTHEW 15:3-9; MARK 7:6-13

The scribes and the Pharisees sit on Moses' seat; therefore, do whatever they teach you and follow it; but do not do as they do, for they do not practice what they teach. They tie up heavy burdens, hard to bear, and lay them on the shoulders of others; but they themselves are unwilling to lift a finger to move them. They do all their deeds to be seen by others; for they make their phylacteries [little leather boxes containing scriptures] broad and their fringes long. They love to have the place of honor at banquets and the best seats in the synagogues, and to be greeted with respect in the marketplaces, and to have people call them rabbi.

— MATTHEW 23:2-7

But woe to you, scribes and Pharisees, hypocrites! For you lock people out of the kingdom of heaven. For you do not go in yourselves, and when others are going in, you stop them.

— MATTHEW 23:13

Beware of the scribes, who like to walk around in long robes, and to be greeted with respect in the marketplaces, and to have the best seats in the synagogues and places of honor in banquets! They devour your widows' houses and for the sake of appearance say long prayers. They will receive the greater condemnation.

— MARK 12:38-40; LUKE 20:46-47; MATTHEW 23:14

Woe to you, scribes and Pharisees, hypocrites! For you cross sea and land to make a single convert, and you make the new convert twice as much a child of hell as yourselves.

— MATTHEW 23:15

Woe to you, blind guides, who say, "Whoever swears by the sanctuary is bound by nothing, but whoever swears by the gold of the sanctuary is bound by the oath." You blind fools! For which is greater, the gold or the sanctuary that has made the gold sacred? And you say, "Whoever swears by the altar is bound by nothing, but whoever swears by the gift that is on the altar is bound by the oath." How blind you are! For which is greater, the gift or the altar that makes the gift sacred? So whoever swears by the altar, swears by it and by everything on it; and whoever swears by the sanctuary, swears by it and by the one who dwells in it; and whoever swears by heaven, swears by the throne of God and by the one who is seated upon it.                    — MATTHEW 23:16-22

Every plant that my heavenly Father has not planted will be uprooted. Let [the Pharisees] alone; they are blind guides of the blind. And if one blind person guides another, both will fall into a pit.

— MATTHEW 15:13-14; LUKE 6:39

Woe to you, scribes and Pharisees, hypocrites! For you clean the outside of the cup and of the plate, but inside they are full of greed and self-indulgence. You blind Pharisee! First clean the inside of the cup [and of the plate], so that the outside also may become clean.

— MATTHEW 23:25-26; LUKE 11:39

You fools! Did not the one who made the outside make the inside also? So give for alms those things that are within; and see, everything will be clean for you.

– Luke 11:40-41

Woe to you, scribes and Pharisees, hypocrites! For you are like whitewashed tombs, which on the outside look beautiful, but inside they are full of the bones of the dead and of all kinds of filth. So you also on the outside look righteous to others, but inside you are full of hypocrisy and lawlessness. – Matthew 23:27-28

You have heard that it was said, "You shall not commit adultery." But I say to you that everyone who looks at a woman with lust has already committed adultery with her in his heart. – Matthew 5:27-28

If your right eye causes you to sin, tear it out and throw it away; it is better for you to lose one of your members than for your whole body to be thrown into hell. And if your right hand causes you to sin, cut it off and throw it away; it is better for you to lose one of your members than for your whole body to go into hell.

– Matthew 5:29-30, 18:8-9; Mark 9:43; cf. 9:45, 47

[To the disciples:] You are the salt of the earth; but if salt has lost its taste, how can its saltiness be restored? It is no longer good for anything, but is thrown out and trampled under foot.

> – MATTHEW 5:13; LUKE 14:34-35; MARK 9:49-50

Have you not read that the one who made them at the beginning "made them male and female," and said, "For this reason a man shall leave his father and mother and be joined to his wife, and the two shall become one flesh"? So they are no longer two, but one flesh. Therefore what God has joined together, let no one separate.

> – MATTHEW 19:4-6; MARK 10:6-9

You have never heard his [the Father's] voice or seen his form, and you do not have his word abiding in you, because you do not believe him whom he has sent.

You search the scriptures because you think that in them you have eternal life; and it is they that testify on my behalf. Yet you refuse to come to me to have life. I do not accept glory from human beings. But I know that you do not have the love of God in you. I have come in my Father's name, and you do not accept me; if another comes in his own name, you will accept him. How can you believe when you accept glory from one another and do not seek the glory that comes from the one who alone is God? Do not think that I will accuse you before the Father; your accuser is Moses, on whom you have set your hope. If you believed Moses, you would believe me, for he wrote about me. But if you do not believe what he wrote, how will you believe what I say?

– John 5:37-47

I am the true vine, and my Father is the vinegrower. He removes every branch in me that bears no fruit. Every branch that bears fruit he prunes to make it bear more fruit. You have already been cleansed by the word that I have spoken to you. Abide in me as I abide in you. Just as the branch cannot bear fruit by itself unless it abides in the vine, neither can you unless you abide in me. I am the vine, you are the branches. Those who abide in me and I in them bear much fruit, because apart from me you can do nothing. Whoever does not abide in me is thrown away like a branch and withers; such branches are gathered, thrown into the fire, and burned.

– John 15:1-6

You [Pharisees] know neither me nor my Father. If you knew me, you would know my Father also.

– John 8:19

Woe to you, scribes and Pharisees, hypocrites! For you build the tombs of the prophets and decorate the graves of the righteous, and you say, "If we had lived in the days of our ancestors, we would not have taken part with them in shedding the blood of the prophets." Thus you testify against yourselves that you are descendants of those who murdered the prophets. Fill up, then, the measure of your ancestors. You snakes, you brood of vipers! How can you escape being sentenced to hell? Therefore I send you prophets, sages, and scribes, some of whom you will kill and crucify, and some you will flog in your synagogues and pursue from town to town, so that upon you may come all the righteous blood shed on earth, from the blood of righteous Abel to the blood of Zechariah son of Barachiah, whom you murdered between the sanctuary and the altar. Truly I tell you, all this will come upon this generation.

– MATTHEW 23:29-36; LUKE 11:47-51

But woe to you Pharisees! For you tithe mint and rue and herbs of all kinds, and neglect justice and the love of God; it is these you ought to have practiced, without neglecting the others. Woe to you Pharisees! For you love to have the seat of honor in the synagogues and to be greeted with respect in the marketplaces. Woe to you! For you are like unmarked graves, and people walk over them without realizing it.

– LUKE 11:42-44; MATTHEW 23:23

You blind guides! You strain out a gnat [which had

fallen into the wine that was to be drunk] but swallow a camel!

— MATTHEW 23:24

I have told you, and you do not believe. The works that I do in my Father's name testify to me; but you do not believe, because you do not belong to my sheep.

— JOHN 10:25-26

[Some Pharisees said, "Surely we are not blind, are we?"] If you were blind, you would not have sin. But now that you say, "We see," your sin remains.

— JOHN 9:41

You are those who justify yourselves in the sight of others; but God knows your hearts; for what is prized by human beings is an abomination in the sight of God.

— LUKE 16:15

But woe to you who are rich, for you have received your consolation.

— LUKE 6:24

Truly I tell you, it will be hard for a rich person to enter the kingdom of heaven. Again I tell you, it is easier for a camel to go through the eye of a needle than for someone who is rich to enter the kingdom of God.

— MATTHEW 19:23-24; MARK 10:23-25; LUKE 18:24-25

Take care! Be on your guard against all kinds of greed;

for one's life does not consist in the abundance of possessions.

— LUKE 12:15

The land of a rich man produced abundantly. And he thought to himself, "What should I do, for I have no place to store my crops?" Then he said, "I will do this: I will pull down my barns and build larger ones, and there I will store all my grain and my goods. And I will say to my soul, 'Soul, you have ample goods laid up for many years; relax, eat, drink, be merry.'" But God said to him, "You fool! This very night your life is being demanded of you. And the things you have prepared, whose will they be?" So it is with those who store up treasures for themselves but are not rich toward God.

— LUKE 12:16-21

Woe to you who are full now, for you will be hungry.

— LUKE 6:25

Woe to you who are laughing now, for you will mourn and weep.

— LUKE 6:25

Woe to you when all speak well of you, for that is what their ancestors did to the false prophets.

— LUKE 6:26

Is it not written,

> "My house [the temple] shall be called a house
> of prayer for all the nations"?

But you have made it a den of robbers.

> – MARK 11:17; MATTHEW 21:13; LUKE 19:46

Take these things [that they were selling] out of here!
Stop making my Father's house a marketplace!

> – JOHN 2:16

You brood of vipers! How can you speak good things,
when you are evil? For out of the abundance of the heart
the mouth speaks. The good person brings good things
out of a good treasure, and the evil person brings evil
things out of an evil treasure. I tell you, on the day of
judgment you will have to give an account for every
careless word you utter; for by your words you will be
justified, and by your words you will be condemned.

> – MATTHEW 12:34-37; LUKE 6:45

Listen to me, all of you, and understand: there is nothing outside a person that by going in can defile, but the
things that come out are what defile.... Then do you
also fail to understand? Do you not see that whatever
goes into a person from outside cannot defile, since it
enters, not the heart but the stomach, and goes out into
the sewer?... It is what comes out of a person that

defiles. For it is from within, from the human heart, that evil intentions come: fornication, theft, murder, adultery, avarice, wickedness, deceit, licentiousness, envy, slander, pride, folly. All these evil things come from within, and they defile a person.

— MARK 7:14-25, 18:23; MATTHEW 15:10-11, 16-19

These are what defile a person, but to eat with unwashed hands does not defile.

— MATTHEW 15:20

Occasions for stumbling [yielding to temptation] are bound to come, but woe to anyone by whom they come! It would be better for you if a millstone were hung around your neck and you were thrown into the sea than for you to cause one of these little ones [disciples] to stumble.

— LUKE 17:1-2; MATTHEW 18:6; CF. 18:7; MARK 9:42

Again it is written,

"Do not put the Lord your God to the test."

— MATTHEW 4:7; LUKE 4:12

Beware of false prophets, who come to you in sheep's clothing but inwardly are ravenous wolves. You will know them by their fruits. Are grapes gathered from thorns, or figs from thistles? In the same way, every good tree bears good fruit, but the bad tree bears bad fruit. A good tree cannot bear bad fruit, nor can a bad tree bear good fruit. Every tree that does not bear good fruit is cut down and thrown into the fire. Thus you will know them by their fruits.

– MATTHEW 7:15-20, 12:33; LUKE 6:43-44; CF. 13:6-9

Why do you see the speck in your neighbor's eye, but do not notice the log in your own eye? Or how can you say to your neighbor, "Friend, let me take out the speck in your eye," when you yourself do not see the log in your own eye? You hypocrite, first take the log out of your own eye, and then you will see clearly to take the speck out of your neighbor's eye.

– LUKE 6:41-42; MATTHEW 7:3-5

Get behind me, Satan! You are a stumbling block to me; for you are setting your mind not on divine things but on human things.

– MATTHEW 16:23; MARK 8:33

Away with you, Satan! for it is written,

> "Worship the Lord your God,
>      and serve only him."

– MATTHEW 4:10; LUKE 4:8

When the unclean spirit has gone out of a person, it

wanders through waterless regions looking for a resting place, but it finds none. Then it says, "I will return to my house from which I came." When he comes, he finds it empty, swept, and put in order. Then it goes and brings along seven other spirits more evil than itself, and they enter and live there; and the last state of that person is worse than the first. So will it be also with this evil generation. — MATTHEW 12:43-45; LUKE 11:24-26

[To the charge that he casts out demons by Beelzebul, ruler of demons:] Every kingdom divided against itself is laid waste, and no city or house divided against itself will stand. If Satan casts out Satan, he is divided against himself; how then will his kingdom stand? If I cast out demons by Beelzebul, by whom do your own exorcists [disciples] cast them out? Therefore they will be your judges.

— MATTHEW 12:25-27; MARK 3:23-26; LUKE 11:17-19

Whoever is not with me is against me, and whoever does not gather with me scatters.

— MATTHEW 12:30; LUKE 11:23

When a strong man, fully armed, guards his castle, his property is safe. But when one stronger than he attacks him and overpowers him, he takes away his armor in which he trusted and divides his plunder.

— LUKE 11:21-22

Therefore I tell you, people will be forgiven for every sin and blasphemy, but blasphemy against the Spirit will not be forgiven. Whoever speaks a word against the Son of Man will be forgiven, but whoever speaks against the Holy Spirit will not be forgiven, either in this age or in the age to come.

— MATTHEW 12:31-32; MARK 3:28-29; LUKE 12:10

Anyone who does not honor the Son does not honor the Father who sent him.

— JOHN 5:23

You have heard that it was said to those of ancient times, "You shall not murder"; and "whoever murders shall be liable to judgment [of the local Jewish court]." But I say to you that if you are angry with a brother or sister, you will be liable to judgment; and if you insult a brother or sister, you will be liable to the council [Sanhedrin]; and if you say, "You fool," you will be liable to the hell of fire.

— MATTHEW 5:21-22

Why do you not understand what I say? It is because you cannot accept my word. You are from your father the devil, and you choose to do your father's desires. He was a murderer from the beginning and does not stand in the truth, because there is no truth in him. When he lies, he speaks according to his own nature, for he is a liar and the father of lies. But because I tell the truth, you do not believe me. Which of you convicts me of sin? If I tell the truth, why do you not believe me? Whoever is from God hears the words of God. The reason you do not hear them is that you are not from God.

– JOHN 8:43-47

[To the church in Ephesus:] These are the words of him who holds the seven stars in his right hand, who walks among the seven golden lampstands:

I know your works, your toil and your patient endurance. I know that you cannot tolerate evildoers; you have tested those who claim to be apostles but are not, and have found them to be false. I also know that you are enduring patiently and bearing up for the sake of my name, and that you have not grown weary. But I have this against you, that you have abandoned the love you had at first. Remember then from what you have fallen; repent, and do the works you did at first. If not, I will come to you and remove your lampstand from its place, unless you repent. Yet this is to your credit: you hate the works of the Nicolaitans, which I also hate. Let anyone who has an ear listen to what the Spirit is saying to the churches. To everyone who conquers, I will give permission to eat from the tree of life that is in the paradise of God.

– REVELATION 2:1-7

[And to the church in Smyrna:] These are the words of the first and the last, who was dead and came to life:

I know your affliction and your poverty, even though you are rich. I know the slander on the part of those who say that they are Jews and are not, but are a synagogue of Satan. Do not fear what you are about to suffer. Beware, the devil is about to throw some of you into prison so that you may be tested, and for ten days you will have affliction. Be faithful until death, and I will give you the crown of life. Let anyone who has an ear listen to what the Spirit is saying to the churches. Whoever conquers will not be harmed by the second death [final condemnation of sinners].

– REVELATION 2:8-11

[And to the church in Pergamum:] These are the words of him who has the sharp two-edged sword:

I know where you are living, where Satan's throne is. Yet you are holding fast to my name, and you did not deny your faith in me even in the days of Antipas my witness, my faithful one, who was killed among you, where Satan lives. But I have a few things against you: you have some there who hold to the teaching of

Balaam, who taught Balak to put a stumbling block
before the people of Israel, so that they would eat food
sacrificed to idols and practice fornication. So you also
have some who hold to the teaching of the Nicolaitans.
Repent then. If not, I will come to you soon and make
war against them with the sword of my mouth. Let anyone who has an ear listen to what the Spirit is saying to
the churches. To everyone who conquers I will give
some of the hidden manna, and I will give a white stone,
and on the white stone is written a new name that no
one knows except the one who receives it.

– REVELATION 2:12-17

[And to the church in Thyatira:] These are the words of
the Son of God, who has eyes like a flame of fire, and
whose feet are like burnished bronze:

I know your works — your love, faith, service, and
patient endurance. I know that your last works are
greater than the first. But I have this against you: you
tolerate that woman Jezebel, who calls herself a prophet
and is teaching and beguiling my servants to practice
fornication and to eat food sacrificed to idols. I gave her
time to repent, but she refuses to repent of her fornication. Beware, I am throwing her on a bed, and those
who commit adultery with her I am throwing into great
distress, unless they repent of her doings; and I will

strike her children dead. And all the churches will know that I am the one who searches minds and hearts, and I will give to each of you as your works deserve. But to the rest of you in Thyatira, who do not hold this teaching, who have not learned what some call "the deep things of Satan [heretical teachings]," to you I say, I do not lay on you any other burden; only hold fast to what you have until I come. To everyone who conquers and continues to do my works to the end,

I will give authority over the nations;
to rule them with an iron rod,

as when clay pots are shattered —

even as I also received authority from my Father. To the one who conquers I will also give the morning star [Christ Himself]. Let anyone who has an ear listen to what the Spirit is saying to the churches.

— REVELATION 2:18-29

[And to the church in Sardis:] These are the words of him who has the seven spirits of God and the seven stars:

I know your works; you have a name of being alive, but you are dead. Wake up, and strengthen what remains and is on the point of death, for I have not found your works perfect in the sight of my God.

Remember then what you received and heard; obey it, and repent. If you do not wake up, I will come like a thief, and you will not know at what hour I will come to you. Yet you have still a few persons in Sardis who have not soiled their clothes; they will walk with me, dressed in white, for they are worthy. If you conquer, you will be clothed like them in white robes, and I will not blot your name out of the book of life; I will confess your name before my Father and before his angels. Let anyone who has an ear listen to what the Spirit is saying to the churches.

— REVELATION 3:1-6

[And to the church in Philadelphia:]

> These are the words of the holy one, the true one,
> > who has the key of David,
> > who opens and no one will shut,
> > who shuts and no one opens:

I know your works. Look, I have set before you an open door, which no one is able to shut. I know that you have but little power, and yet you have kept my word and have not denied my name. I will make those of the synagogue of Satan who say that they are Jews and are not, but are lying — I will make them come and bow down before your feet, and they will learn that I have loved you. Because you have kept my word of patient endurance, I will keep you from the hour of trial that is coming on the whole world to test the inhabitants of the earth. I am coming soon; hold fast to what you have, so that no one may seize your crown. If you conquer, I will make you a pillar in the temple of my God; you will never go out of it. I will write on you the name of my God, and the name of the city of my God, the new Jerusalem that comes down from my God out of heaven, and my own new name. Let anyone who has an ear listen to what the Spirit is saying to the churches.

– REVELATION 3:7-13

[And to the church in Laodicea:] The words of the Amen, the faithful and true witness, the origin of God's creation:

I know your works; you are neither cold nor hot. I wish that you were either cold or hot. So, because you are lukewarm, and neither cold nor hot, I am about to spit you out of my mouth. For you say, "I am rich, I have prospered, and I need nothing." You do not realize that you are wretched, pitiable, poor, blind, and naked. Therefore I counsel you to buy from me gold refined by fire so that you may be rich; and white robes to clothe you and to keep the shame of your nakedness from being seen; and salve to anoint your eyes so that you may see. I reprove and discipline those whom I love. Be earnest, therefore, and repent. Listen! I am standing at the door, knocking; if you hear my voice and open the door, I will come in to you and eat with you, and you with me. To the one who conquers I will give a place with me on my throne, just as I myself conquered and sat down with my Father on his throne. Let anyone who has an ear listen to what the Spirit is saying to the churches.

— REVELATION 3:14-22

And everyone who hears these words of mine and does not act on them will be like a foolish man who built his house on sand. The rain fell, and the floods came, and the winds blew and beat against that house, and it fell — and great was its fall!

— MATTHEW 7:26-27; LUKE 6:49

# Signs of
# The End

Very truly, I tell you, the hour is coming, and is now here, when the [spiritually] dead will hear the voice of the Son of God, and those who hear will live. For just as the Father has life in himself, so he has granted the Son also to have life in himself; and he has given him authority to execute judgment, because he is the Son of Man. Do not be astonished at this; for the hour is coming when all who are in their graves will hear his voice and will come out — those who have done good, to the resurrection of life, and those who have done evil, to the resurrection of condemnation.

– John 5:25-29

For the Son of Man is to come with his angels in the glory of his Father, and then he will repay everyone for what has been done. Truly I tell you, there are some standing here who will not taste death before they see the Son of Man coming in his kingdom.

– MATTHEW 16:27-28; MARK 9:1; LUKE 9:27

Woman [of Samaria], believe me, the hour is coming when you will worship the Father neither on this mountain [Gerizim] nor in Jerusalem. You worship what you do not know; we worship what we know, for salvation is from the Jews. But the hour is coming, and is now here, when the true worshipers will worship the Father in spirit and truth, for the Father seeks such as these to worship him.

– JOHN 4:21-23

Daughters of Jerusalem, do not weep for me, but weep for yourselves and for your children. For the days are surely coming when they will say, "Blessed are the barren, and the wombs that never bore, and the breasts that never nursed." Then they will begin to say to the mountains, "Fall on us"; and to the hills, "Cover us." For if they do this when the wood is green, what will happen when it is dry?

– LUKE 23:28-31

So when you see the desolating sacrilege [of Jerusalem] standing in the holy place, as was spoken of by the prophet Daniel ... then those in Judea must flee to the mountains; the one on the housetop must not go down to take what is in the house; the one in the field must not turn back to get a coat. Woe to those who are pregnant and to those who are nursing infants in those days! Pray that your flight may not be in winter or on a sabbath. For at that time there will be great suffering, such as has not been from the beginning of the world until now, no, and never will be. And if those days had not been cut short, no one would be saved; but for the sake of the elect those days will be cut short.

– MATTHEW 24:15-22; MARK 13:14-20; LUKE 21:20-24

Beware that no one leads you astray. For many will come in my name, saying, "I am the Christ!" and they will lead many astray. And you will hear of wars and rumors of wars; see that you are not alarmed; for this must take place, but the end is not yet. For nation will rise against nation, and kingdom against kingdom, and there will be famines and earthquakes in various places: all this is but the beginning of the birth pangs.

– MATTHEW 24:4-8; MARK 13:5-8; LUKE 21:8-11

And if anyone says to you at that time, "Look! Here is the Christ!" or "Look! There he is!" — do not believe it. False Christs and false prophets will appear and produce signs and omens, to lead astray, if possible, the elect. But be alert; I have already told you everything.

— MARK 13:21-23

The days are coming when you will long to see one of the days of the Son of Man, and you will not see it. They will say to you, "Look there!" or "Look here!" Do not go, do not set off in pursuit. For as the lightning flashes and lights up the sky from one side to the other, so will the Son of Man be in his day. But first he must endure much suffering and be rejected by this generation. Just as it was in the days of Noah, so too it will be in the days of the Son of Man. They were eating and drinking, and marrying and being given in marriage, until the day Noah entered the ark, and the flood came and destroyed all of them. Likewise, just as it was in the days of Lot: they were eating and drinking, buying and selling, planting and building, but on the day that Lot left Sodom, it rained fire and sulfur from heaven and destroyed all of them — it will be like that on the day that the Son of Man is revealed. On that day, anyone on the housetop who has belongings in the house must not come down to take them away; and likewise anyone in the field must not turn back. Remember Lot's wife. Those who try to make their life secure will lose it, but those who lose their life will keep it. I tell you, on that night there will be two in one bed; one will be taken and the other left. There will be two women grinding meal together; one will be taken and the other left.

– LUKE 17:22-36; MATTHEW 24:23-28, 37-41

Be dressed for action and have your lamps lit; be like those who are waiting for their master to return from the wedding banquet, so that they may open the door for him as soon as he comes and knocks. Blessed are those slaves whom the master finds alert when he comes; truly I tell you, he will fasten his belt and have them sit down to eat, and he will come and serve them. If he comes during the middle of the night, or near dawn, and finds them so, blessed are those slaves.

– LUKE 12:35-38

But about that day and hour no one knows, neither the angels of heaven, nor the Son, but only the Father.... Keep awake therefore, for you do not know on what day your Lord is coming. But understand this: if the owner of the house had known in what part of the night the thief was coming, he would have stayed awake and would not have let his house be broken into. Therefore you also must be ready, for the Son of Man is coming at an unexpected hour.

– MATTHEW 24:36, 42-44; LUKE 12:39-40

See, I am coming like a thief! Blessed is the one who stays awake and is clothed, not going about naked and exposed to shame.

— REVELATION 16:15

Beware, keep alert; for you do not know when the time will come. It is like a man going on a journey, when he leaves home and puts his slaves in charge, each with his work, and commands the doorkeeper to be on the watch. Therefore, keep awake — for you do not know when the master of the house will come, in the evening [9:00 P.M.], or at midnight, or at cockcrow [3:00 A.M.], or at dawn [6:00 A.M.], or else he may find you asleep when he comes suddenly. And what I say to you I say to all: Keep awake.

— MARK 13:33-37

There will be signs in the sun, the moon, and the stars, and on the earth distress among nations confused by the roaring of the sea and the waves. People will faint from fear and foreboding of what is coming upon the world, for the powers of the heavens will be shaken. Then they will see "the Son of Man coming in a cloud" with power and great glory. Now when these things begin to take place, stand up and raise your heads, because your redemption is drawing near.

— LUKE 21:25-28

Immediately after the suffering of those days

> the sun will be darkened,
> and the moon will not give its light;

> the stars will fall from heaven,
>> and the powers of the heavens
>> will be shaken.

Then the sign of the Son of Man will appear in heaven, and then all the tribes of the earth will mourn, and they will see "the Son of Man coming on the clouds of heaven" with power and great glory. And he will send out his angels with a loud trumpet call, and they will gather his elect from the four winds, from one end of heaven to the other. — MATTHEW 24:29-31; MARK 13:24-27

From the fig tree learn its lesson: as soon as its branch becomes tender and puts forth its leaves, you know that summer is near. So also, when you see all these things, you know that it is near, at the very gates. Truly I tell you, this generation will not pass away until all these things have taken place.

— MATTHEW 24:32-34; MARK 13:28-30; LUKE 21:29-32

When you see a cloud rising in the west, you immediately say, "It is going to rain"; and so it happens. And when you see the south wind blowing, you say, "There will be scorching heat"; and it happens. You hypocrites! You know how to interpret the appearance of earth and sky, but why do you not know how to interpret the present time? — LUKE 12:54-56; CF. MATTHEW 16:2-3

For just as Jonah was three days and three nights in the belly of the sea monster, so for three days and three nights the Son of Man will be in the heart of the earth. The people of Nineveh will rise up at the judgment with this generation and condemn it, because they repented at the proclamation of Jonah, and see, something greater than Jonah is here! The queen of the South [Queen of Sheba] will rise up at the judgment with this generation and condemn it, because she came from the ends of the earth to listen to the wisdom of Solomon, and see, something greater than Solomon is here!

– MATTHEW 12:40-42; LUKE 11:30-32

An evil and adulterous generation asks for a sign, but no sign will be given to it except the sign of Jonah.

MATTHEW 16:4, 12:39; LUKE 11:29; CF. MARK 8:12

Be on guard so that your hearts are not weighed down with dissipation and drunkenness and the worries of this life, and that day catch you unexpectedly, like a trap. For it will come upon all who live on the face of the whole earth. Be alert at all times, praying that you may have the strength to escape all these things that will take place, and to stand before the Son of Man.

– LUKE 21:34-36

A man planted a vineyard, put a fence around it, dug a pit for the wine press, and built a watchtower; then he leased it to tenants and went to another country. When the season came, he sent a slave to the tenants to collect from them his share of the produce of the vineyard. But they seized him, and beat him, and sent him away empty-handed. And again he sent another slave to them; this one they beat over the head and insulted. Then he sent another, and that one they killed. And so it was with many others; some they beat, and others they killed. He had still one other, a beloved son. Finally he sent him to them, saying, "They will respect my son." But those tenants said to one another, "This is the heir; come, let us kill him, and the inheritance will be ours." So they seized him, killed him, and threw him out of the vineyard. What then will the owner of the vineyard do? He will come and destroy the tenants and give the vineyard to others. Have you not read this scripture:

> "The stone that the builders rejected
> has become the head of the
> cornerstone;
> this was the Lord's doing,
> and it is amazing in our eyes"?

– Mark 12:1-11; Matthew 21:33-40, 42; Luke 20:9-17

Everyone who falls on that stone will be broken to pieces; and it will crush anyone on whom it falls.

– Luke 20:18; Matthew 21:44

You see all these [buildings of the temple], do you not? Truly I tell you, not one stone will be left here upon another; all will be thrown down.

— MATTHEW, 24:2; MARK 13:2; LUKE 21:6

Therefore I tell you, the kingdom of God will be taken away from you and given to a people that produces the fruits of the kingdom.

— MATTHEW 21:43

I did not say these things to you from the beginning, because I was with you. But now I am going to him who sent me; yet none of you asks me, "Where are you going?" But because I have said these things to you, sorrow has filled your hearts. Nevertheless I tell you the truth: it is to your advantage that I go away, for if I do not go away, the Advocate [the Holy Spirit] will not come to you; but if I go, I will send him to you. And when he comes, he will prove the world wrong about sin and righteousness and judgment: about sin, because they do not believe in me; about righteousness, because I am going to the Father, and you will see me no longer; about judgment, because the ruler of this world has been condemned.

— JOHN 16:4-11

Very truly, I tell you, you will see heaven opened and the angels of God ascending and descending upon the Son of Man.

— JOHN 1:51

If you [Jerusalem], even you, had only recognized on this day the things that make for peace! But now they are hidden from your eyes. Indeed, the days will come upon you, when your enemies will set up ramparts around you and surround you, and hem you in on every side. They will crush you to the ground, you and your children [the city's inhabitants] within you, and they will not leave within you one stone upon another; because you did not recognize the time of your visitation from God.

– LUKE 19:42-44

Woe to you, Chorazin! Woe to you, Bethsaida! For if the deeds of power done in you had been done in Tyre and Sidon, they would have repented long ago in sackcloth and ashes. But I tell you, on the day of judgment it will be more tolerable for Tyre and Sidon than for you. And you, Capernaum, will you be exalted to heaven? No, you will be brought down to Hades. For if the deeds of power done in you had been done in Sodom, it would have remained until this day. But I tell you that on the day of judgment it will be more tolerable for the land of Sodom than for you.

– MATTHEW 11:21-24; LUKE 10:13-15

# DISCIPLESHIP

# THE CALL

F ollow me.
— JOHN 1:43; MATTHEW 9:9; MARK 2:14; LUKE 5:27, 9:59

Follow me and I will make you fish for people.
— MARK 1:17; MATTHEW 4:19

It is not for you to know the times or periods that the Father has set by his own authority. But you will receive power when the Holy Spirit has come upon you; and you will be my witnesses in Jerusalem, in all Judea and Samaria, and to the ends of the earth.
— ACTS 1:7-8

[Simon Peter said, "You are the Christ, the Son of the living God."] Blessed are you, Simon son of Jonah! For flesh and blood has not revealed this to you, but my

Father in heaven. And I tell you, you are Peter, and on this rock I will build my church, and the gates of Hades will not prevail against it. I will give you the keys of the kingdom of heaven, and whatever you bind on earth will be bound in heaven, and whatever you loose on earth will be loosed in heaven.

— MATTHEW 16:17-19; 18:18

Simon son of John, do you love me more than these [other disciples]?... Feed my lambs.... Simon son of John, do you love me?... Tend my sheep.... Simon son of John, do you love me?... Feed my sheep. Very truly, I tell you, when you were younger, you used to fasten your own belt and to go wherever you wished. But when you grow old, you will stretch out your hands, and someone else will fasten a belt around you and take you where you do not wish to go [martyred under Nero at Rome].... Follow me.

— JOHN 21:15-19

Saul, Saul, why do you persecute me?... I am Jesus, whom you are persecuting. But get up and enter the city [Damascus], and you will be told what you are to do.

— ACTS 9:4-6; CF. 26:14-15

I have appeared to you [Saul] for this purpose, to appoint you to serve and testify to the things in which you have seen me and to those in which I will appear to you. I will rescue you from your people and from the Gentiles — to whom I am sending you to open their eyes so that they may turn from darkness to light and from the power of Satan to God, so that they may receive forgiveness of sins and a place among those who are sanctified by faith in me.

— ACTS 26:16-18

[To Ananias, a disciple in Damascus:] Get up and go to the street called Straight, and at the house of Judas look for a man of Tarsus named Saul. At this moment he is praying, and he has seen in a vision a man named Ananias come in and lay his hands on him so that he might regain his sight. . . . Go, for he is an instrument whom I have chosen to bring my name before Gentiles and kings and before the people of Israel; I myself will show him how much he must suffer for the sake of my name.

— ACTS 9:11-12, 15-16

[To Paul:] Do not be afraid, but speak and do not be silent; for I am with you, and no one will lay a hand on you to harm you, for there are many in this city [Corinth] who are my people.

— ACTS 18:9-10

Whoever welcomes you welcomes me, and whoever welcomes me welcomes the one who sent me.

— MATTHEW 10:40; MARK 9:37

Whoever listens to you listens to me, and whoever rejects you rejects me, and whoever rejects me rejects the one who sent me.

— LUKE 10:16

[Quoting from the prophet Isaiah:] "I have set you to be a light for the Gentiles, so that you may bring salvation to the ends of the earth."

— ACTS 13:47

You did not choose me but I chose you. And I appointed you to go and bear fruit, fruit that will last, so that the Father will give you whatever you ask him in my name. I am giving you these commands so that you may love one another.

— JOHN 15:16-17

[Regarding a man casting out demons in Christ's name:] Do not stop him; for no one who does a deed of power in my name will be able soon afterward to speak evil of me. Whoever is not against us is for us. For truly I tell you, whoever gives you a cup of water to drink because you bear the name of Christ will by no means lose the reward.

— MARK 9:39-41; LUKE 9:50

Let the [spiritually] dead bury their own dead; but as for you, go and proclaim the kingdom of God.... No one who puts a hand to the plow and looks back is fit for the kingdom of God.

— LUKE 9:60, 62; MATTHEW 8:22

I watched Satan fall from heaven like a flash of lightning. See, I have given you authority to tread on snakes and scorpions, and over all the power of the enemy; and nothing will hurt you. Nevertheless, do not rejoice at this, that the spirits submit to you, but rejoice that your names are written in heaven.

— LUKE 10:18-20

Go into all the world and proclaim the good news to the whole creation. The one who believes and is baptized will be saved; but the one who does not believe will be condemned. And these signs will accompany those who believe: by using my name they will cast out demons; they will speak in new tongues; they will pick up snakes in their hands, and if they drink any deadly thing, it will not hurt them; they will lay their hands on the sick, and they will recover.

— MARK 16:15-18

Peace be with you. . . . Peace be with you. As the Father has sent me, so I send you.

— JOHN 20:19, 21

All authority in heaven and on earth has been given to me. Go therefore and make disciples of all nations, baptizing them in the name of the Father and of the Son and of the Holy Spirit, and teaching them to obey everything that I have commanded you. And remember, I am with you always, to the end of the age.

— MATTHEW 28:18-20

# THE RULES

Go nowhere among the Gentiles, and enter no town of the Samaritans, but go rather to the lost sheep of the house of Israel. As you go, proclaim the good news, "The kingdom of heaven is at hand." – MATTHEW 10:5-7

See, I am sending you out like sheep into the midst of wolves; so be wise as serpents and innocent as doves.

– MATTHEW 10:16

In everything do to others as you would have them do to you; for this is the law and the prophets.

– MATTHEW 7:12

It is written, "One does not live by bread alone, but by

every word that comes from the mouth of God."

— MATTHEW 4:4; LUKE 4:4

Whoever comes to me and does not hate father and mother, wife and children, brothers and sisters, yes, and even life itself, cannot be my disciple. Whoever does not carry the cross and follow me cannot be my disciple. For which of you, intending to build a tower, does not first sit down and estimate the cost, to see whether he has enough to complete it? Otherwise, when he has laid a foundation and is not able to finish, all who see it begin to ridicule him, saying, "This fellow began to build and was not able to finish." Or what king, going out to wage war against another king, will not sit down first and consider whether he is able with ten thousand to oppose the one who comes against him with twenty thousand? If he cannot, then, while the other is still far away, he sends a delegation and asks for the terms of peace. So therefore, none of you can become my disciple if you do not give up all your possessions.

— LUKE 14:26-33; CF. MATTHEW 10:37-38

The harvest is plentiful, but the laborers are few; therefore ask the Lord of the harvest to send out laborers into his harvest. Go on your way. See, I am sending you out like lambs into the midst of wolves. Carry no purse, no bag, no sandals; and greet no one on the road. Whatever house you enter, first say, "Peace to this house!" And if anyone is there who shares in peace, your peace will rest on that person; but if not, it will return to you. Remain in the same house, eating and drinking whatever they provide, for the laborer deserves to be paid. Do not move about from house to house. Whenever you enter a town and its people welcome you, eat what is set before you; cure the sick who are there, and say to them, "The kingdom of God has come near to you." But whenever you enter a town and they do not welcome you, go out into its streets and say, "Even the dust of your town that clings to our feet, we wipe off in protest against you. Yet know this: the kingdom of God has come near." I tell you, on that day it will be more tolerable for Sodom than for that town.

– LUKE 10:2-12, 9:3-5;
MATTHEW 9:37-38; 10:8-15; MARK 6:10-11

What I say to you in the dark, tell in the light; and what you hear whispered, proclaim from the housetops.

– MATTHEW 10:27

Cure the sick, raise the dead, cleanse the lepers, cast out demons.

– MATTHEW 10:8

Do not give what is holy to dogs; and do not throw your pearls before swine, or they will trample them under foot and turn and maul you.

— Matthew 7:6; cf. 15:26; Mark 7:27

Who among you would say to your slave who has just come in from plowing or tending sheep in the field, "Come here at once and take your place at the table"? Would you not rather say to him, "Prepare supper for me, put on your apron and serve me while I eat and drink; later you may eat and drink"? Do you thank the slave for doing what was commanded? So you also, when you have done all that you were ordered [by God] to do, say, "We are worthless slaves; we have done only what we ought to have done!"

— Luke 17:7-10

When you are invited by someone to a wedding banquet, do not sit down at the place of honor, in case someone more distinguished than you has been invited by your host; and the host who invited both of you may come and say to you, "Give this person your place," and then in disgrace you would start to take the lowest place. But when you are invited, go and sit down at the lowest place, so that when your host comes, he may say to you, "Friend, move up higher"; then you will be honored in the presence of all who sit at the table with you. For all who exalt themselves will be humbled, and those who humble themselves will be exalted.

— Luke 14:8-11

Two men went up to the temple to pray, one a Pharisee and the other a tax collector. The Pharisee, standing by himself, was praying thus, "God, I thank you that I am not like other people: thieves, rogues, adulterers, or even like this tax collector. I fast twice a week; I give a tenth of all my income." But the tax collector, standing far off, would not even look up to heaven, but was beating his breast and saying, "God, be merciful to me, a sinner!" I tell you, this man went down to his home justified rather than the other; for all who exalt themselves will be humbled, but all who humble themselves will be exalted.

— LUKE 18:10-14; MATTHEW 23:12

You know that among the Gentiles those whom they recognize as their rulers lord it over them, and their great ones are tyrants over them. But it is not so among you; but whoever wishes to become great among you must be your servant, and whoever wishes to be first among you must be slave of all. For the Son of Man came not to be served but to serve, and to give his life a ransom for many.

— MARK 10:42-45, 9:35; MATTHEW 20:25-28; LUKE 22:25-26

For who is greater, the one who is at the table or the one who serves? Is it not the one at the table? But I am among you as one who serves.

— LUKE 22:27

But you are not to be called rabbi, for you have one teacher, and you are all students. And call no man your father on earth, for you have one Father — the one in heaven. Nor are you to be called instructors, for you have one instructor, the Christ. The greatest among you will be your servant.

— MATTHEW 23:8-11

Bring me a denarius and let me see it. . . . Whose head is this, and whose title? [They answered: "The emperor's."] . . . Give to the emperor [Caesar] the things that are the emperor's, and to God the things that are God's.

— MARK 12:15-17; MATTHEW 22:18-21; LUKE 20:24-25

[To the Pharisees who accuse him of breaking the sabbath:] Have you not read what David did when he and his companions were hungry? He entered the house of God and ate the bread of the Presence, which it was not lawful for him or his companions to eat, but only for the priests. Or have you not read in the law that on the sabbath the priests in the temple break the sabbath and yet are guiltless? I tell you, something greater than the temple is here. But if you had known what this means, "I desire mercy and not sacrifice," you would not have condemned the guiltless. For the Son of Man is lord of the sabbath.

— MATTHEW 12:3-8; MARK 2:25-28; LUKE 6:3-5

Is it lawful to cure people on the sabbath, or not? . . . If one of you has a child or an ox that has fallen into a well, will you not immediately pull it out on a sabbath day?

— LUKE 14:3, 5

Suppose one of you has only one sheep and it falls into a pit on the sabbath; will you not lay hold of it and lift it out? How much more valuable is a human being than a sheep! So it is lawful to do good on the sabbath.

— MATTHEW 12:11-12

Does not each of you on the sabbath untie his ox or his donkey from the manger, and lead it away to give it water? And ought not this woman [crippled by a spirit for eighteen years], a daughter of Abraham whom Satan bound for eighteen long years, be set free from this bondage on the sabbath day?

— LUKE 13:15-16

[To the man with a withered right hand:] Come and stand here.... I ask you, is it lawful to do good or to do harm on the sabbath, to save life or to destroy it?... Stretch out your hand [and his hand was restored].

— LUKE 6:8-10; MARK 3:3-5; MATTHEW 12:13

I performed one work, and all of you are astonished. Moses gave you circumcision (it is, of course, not from Moses, but from the patriarchs), and you circumcise a man on the sabbath. If a man receives circumcision on the sabbath in order that the law of Moses may not be broken, are you angry with me because I healed a man's whole body on the sabbath? Do not judge by appearances, but judge with right judgment. — JOHN 7:21-24

Pay attention to what you hear; the measure [judgment] you give will be the measure you get, and still more will be given you. — MARK 4:24; MATTHEW 7:2; LUKE 6:38

Suppose one of you has a friend, and you go to him at midnight and say to him, "Friend, lend me three loaves of bread; for a friend of mine has arrived, and I have nothing to set before him." And he answers from within, "Do not bother me; the door has already been locked, and my children are with me in bed; I cannot get up and give you anything." I tell you, even though he will not get up and give him anything because he is his friend, at least because of his persistence he will get up and give him whatever he needs. — LUKE 11:5-8

Truly I tell you, this poor widow has put in more than all those who are contributing to the treasury. For all of them have contributed out of their abundance; but she out of her poverty has put in everything she had, all she had to live on. — MARK 12:43-44; LUKE 21:3-4

[Regarding a woman with an alabaster jar of costly ointment:] Let her alone; why do you trouble her? She has performed a good service for me. For you always have the poor with you, and you can show kindness to them whenever you wish; but you will not always have me. She has done what she could; she has anointed my body beforehand for its burial. Truly I tell you, wherever the good news is proclaimed in the whole world, what she has done will be told in remembrance of her.

— MARK 14:6-9; MATTHEW 26:10-13

You have heard that it was said, "An eye for an eye and a tooth for a tooth." But I say to you, Do not resist an evildoer. But if anyone strikes you on the right cheek, turn the other also; and if anyone wants to sue you and take your coat, give him your cloak as well; and if anyone forces you to go one mile, go also the second mile. Give to everyone who begs from you, and do not refuse anyone who wants to borrow from you.

— MATTHEW 5:38-42

When you give a luncheon or a dinner, do not invite your friends or your brothers or your relatives or rich neighbors, in case they may invite you in return, and you would be repaid. But when you give a banquet, invite the poor, the crippled, the lame, and the blind. And you will be blessed, because they cannot repay you, for you will be repaid at the resurrection of the righteous.

— LUKE 14:12-14

Again, you have heard that it was said to those of ancient times, "You shall not swear falsely, but carry out the vows you have made to the Lord." But I say to you, Do not swear at all, either by heaven, for it is the throne of God, or by the earth, for it is his footstool, or by Jerusalem, for it is the city of the great King. And do not swear by your head, for you cannot make one hair white or black. Let your word be "Yes, Yes" or "No, No"; anything more than this comes from the evil one.

— MATTHEW 5:33-37

And whenever you fast, do not look dismal, like the hypocrites, for they disfigure their faces so as to show others that they are fasting. Truly I tell you, they have received their reward. But when you fast, put oil on your head and wash your face, so that your fasting may be seen not by others but by your Father who is in secret; and your Father who sees in secret will reward you.

— MATTHEW 6:16-18

Beware of practicing your piety before others in order to be seen by them; for then you will have no reward from your Father in heaven.

So whenever you give alms, do not sound a trumpet before you, as the hypocrites do in the synagogues and in the streets, so that they may be praised by others. Truly I tell you, they have received their reward. But when you give alms, do not let your left hand know what your right hand is doing, so that your alms may be done in secret; and your Father who sees in secret will reward you.

— Matthew 6:1-4

And whenever you pray, do not be like the hypocrites; for they love to stand and pray in the synagogues and at the street corners, so that they may be seen by others. Truly I tell you, they have received their reward. But whenever you pray, go into your room and shut the door and pray to your Father who is in secret; and your Father who sees in secret will reward you.

When you are praying, do not heap up empty phrases as the Gentiles do; for they think that they will be heard because of their many words. Do not be like them, for your Father knows what you need before you ask him.

— Matthew 6:5-8

Pray then in this way:

> Our Father in heaven,
>     hallowed be your name.

Your kingdom come,
Your will be done,
        on earth as it is in heaven.
Give us this day our daily bread.
And forgive us our debts,
        as we also have forgiven our debtors.
And do not bring us into temptation,
        but rescue us from evil.

— MATTHEW 6:9-13; LUKE 11:2-4

No slave can serve two masters; for a slave will either hate the one and love the other, or be devoted to the one and despise the other. You cannot serve God and wealth.

— LUKE 16:13; MATTHEW 6:24

A man was going down from Jerusalem to Jericho, and fell into the hands of robbers, who stripped him, beat him, and went away, leaving him half dead. Now by chance a priest was going down that road; and when he saw him, he passed by on the other side. So likewise a Levite, when he came to the place and saw him, passed by on the other side. But a Samaritan while traveling came near him; and when he saw him, he was moved with pity. He went to him and bandaged his wounds, having poured oil and wine on them. Then he put him on his own animal, brought him to an inn, and took care of him. The next day he took out two denarii [two days' wages], gave them to the innkeeper, and said, "Take care of him; and when I come back, I will repay you whatever more you spend." Which of these three, do you think, was a neighbor to the man who fell into the hands of the robbers? [The lawyer said, "The one who showed him mercy."] . . . . Go and do likewise.    – LUKE 10:30-37

Come away to a deserted place all by yourselves and rest a while.    – MARK 6:31

# THE COST

D o not think that I have come to bring peace to the earth; I have not come to bring peace, but a sword.

For I have come to set a man against his father, and a daughter against her mother, and a daughter-in-law against her mother-in-law; and one's foes will be members of one's own household.

— MATTHEW 10:34-36; LUKE 12:51-53

[Someone said to him, "I will follow you wherever you go."] Foxes have holes, and birds of the air have nests, but the Son of Man has nowhere to lay his head.

— LUKE 9:58; MATTHEW 8:20

When they persecute you in one town, flee to the next; for truly I tell you, you will not have gone through all the towns of Israel before the Son of Man comes.

– MATTHEW 10:23

Then they will hand you over to be tortured and will put you to death, and you will be hated by all nations because of my name. Then many will fall away, and they will betray one another and hate one another. And many false prophets will arise and lead many astray. And because of the increase of lawlessness, the love of many will grow cold. But the one who endures to the end will be saved. And this good news of the kingdom will be proclaimed throughout the whole world, as a testimony to all the nations; and then the end will come.

– MATTHEW 24:9-14

As for yourselves, beware; for they will hand you over to councils; and you will be beaten in synagogues; and you will stand before governors and kings because of me, as a testimony to them. And the good news must first be proclaimed to all nations. When they bring you to trial and hand you over, do not worry beforehand about what you are to say; but say whatever is given you at that time, for it is not you who speak, but the Holy Spirit. Brother will betray brother to death, and a father his child, and children will rise against parents and have them put to death; and you will be hated by all because

of my name. But the one who endures to the end will be saved.                            — MARK 13:9-13; LUKE 12:11-12, 21:12-19;
MATTHEW 10:17-22

Prophets are not without honor, except in their hometown, and among their own kin, and in their own house.                            — MARK 6:4; MATTHEW 13:57; LUKE 4:24

A disciple is not above the teacher, nor a slave above the master; it is enough for the disciple to be like the teacher, and the slave like the master. If they have called the master of the house Beelzebul, how much more will they malign those of his household!

— MATTHEW 10:24-25; LUKE 6:40

If the world hates you, be aware that it hated me before it hated you. If you belonged to the world, the world would love you as its own. Because you do not belong to the world, but I have chosen you out of the world — therefore the world hates you.                            — JOHN 15:18-19

Remember the word that I said to you, "Servants are not greater than their master." If they persecuted me, they will persecute you; if they kept my word, they will keep yours also. . . . Whoever hates me hates my Father also. If I had not done among them the works that no one else did, they would not have sin. But now they have seen and hated both me and my Father. It was to fulfill the word that is written in their law, "They hated me without a cause."

When the Advocate [the Holy Spirit] comes, whom I will send to you from the Father, the Spirit of truth who comes from the Father, he will testify on my behalf. You also are to testify because you have been with me from the beginning.                    – JOHN 15:20, 23-27

I have said these things to you to keep you from stumbling [yielding to temptation]. They will put you out of the synagogues. Indeed, an hour is coming when those who kill you will think that by doing so they are offering worship to God. And they will do this because they have not known the Father or me. But I have said these things to you so that when their hour comes you may remember that I told you about them.        – JOHN 16:1-4

# AFTERWORD

He was born in an obscure village, the child of a peasant woman. He grew up in still another village, where He worked in a carpenter shop until He was thirty. Then for three years He was an itinerant preacher. He never wrote a book. He never held an office. He never had a family or owned a house. He didn't go to college. He never visited a big city. He never traveled more than two hundred miles from the place where He was born. He did none of the things one usually associates with greatness. He had no credentials but himself.

He was only thirty-three when the tide of public opinion turned against Him. His friends ran away. He was turned over to His enemies and went through the mockery of a trial. He was nailed to a cross between two thieves. While He was dying, His executioners gambled for His clothing, the only property He had on earth. When He was dead, He was laid in a borrowed grave through the pity of a friend.

Nearly twenty centuries have come and gone. . . . All the armies that ever marched, all the navies that ever sailed, all the parliaments that ever sat, all the kings that ever reigned, all of these put together have not affected the lives of people on this earth as much as that *one solitary life*.

— ANONYMOUS

He comes to us as One unknown, without a name, as of old, by the lakeside. He came to those men who knew Him not. He speaks to us the same word: "Follow thou me!" and sets us to the tasks which He has to fulfill for our time. He commands. And to those who obey Him, whether they be wise or simple, He will reveal Himself in the toils, the conflicts, the sufferings which they shall pass through in His fellowship, and, as an ineffable mystery, they shall learn in their own experience Who He is.

— ALBERT SCHWEITZER, 1875-1965<br>GERMAN PHYSICIAN, MISSIONARY, AUTHOR<br>(The Quest for the Historical Jesus, 1936)

[God said:] . . . Consider the bridge that is my Son, and see how its great span reaches from heaven to earth; see, that is, how it links the grandeur of the Godhead with the clay of your humanity....No heaping up of earth alone could ever have sufficed to make a bridge great enough to span the torrent and open the way to eternal life....So my sublimity stooped to the earth of your humanity and together they made a bridge and remade the road. And why? So that you might indeed come to the joy of the angels. But it would be no use my Son's having become your bridge to life if you do not use it.

— CATHERINE OF SIENA, 1347-1380
ITALIAN DOMINICAN NUN
(*The Dialogue of Divine Providence, circa* 1369)

"Either God exists, or he does not." But which side shall we take? Reason cannot decide for us one way or the other; we are separated by an infinite gulf. A game is on, at the other side of this infinite distance, where either heads or tails will turn up. Which will you gamble on?...

Let us weigh the gain and the loss in betting that God exists....If you win, you win everything; if you lose, you lose nothing. Do not hesitate, then: gamble on his existence....

You want to come to faith, but you do not know the way. You would like to cure yourself of unbelief, and you ask for remedies. Learn from those who were once bound and gagged like you, and who now stake all that they possess. These are the people who know the road you wish to follow; they are cured of the disease of which you wish to be cured. Follow the way by which they set out: by acting as though they already believed . . . .

Now what harm will come to you if you follow this course? You will be faithful, honest, humble, grateful, generous, a sincere friend, truthful. Certainly you will not enjoy those poisonous pleasures, ambition and luxury. But will you not have others? I tell you that you will gain in this life, and that at every step you take along this road you will see so great an assurance of gain, and so little in what you risk, that you will finally realize you have gambled on something certain and infinite, which has cost you nothing.           — BLAISE PASCAL, 1623-1662
FRENCH MATHEMATICIAN, PHYSICIST, MORALIST
("The Wager," *Pensées*, 1670)

# About the Editor

Dale Salwak, a professor of English at Southern California's Citrus College, has taught courses and conducted seminars on biblical history and literature for over twenty years. He was educated at Purdue University and then the University of Southern California under a National Defense Education Act competitive fellowship program. In 1985 he was awarded a National Endowment for the Humanities grant. In 1987 Purdue University awarded him its Distinguished Alumni Award. He is widely published; his works include sixteen books on various contemporary literary figures as well as *The Wonders of Solitude* (New World Library).

# ACKNOWLEDGMENTS

For their generous help with this project I am indebted especially to the following good people: Dr. Reginald Clarke, Laura Nagy, my parents Dr. Stanley and Frances H. Salwak, and my wife Patti. I would also like to acknowledge Dr. Lloyd John Ogilvie, whose biblical scholarship the past twenty-five years has done so much to clarify and enrich my understanding of Christ's words; and Marc Allen, Becky Benenate, Linda Corwin, and Janet Stark of New World Library for their tireless efforts to see this book through production.